Finding

God

at the

City Dump

The George LeMaster Story

Dan Steinbeck

ISBN 978-1-68517-585-6 (paperback)
ISBN 978-1-68517-586-3 (digital)

Christian Faith Publishing
832 Park Avenue
Meadville, PA 16335
www.christianfaithpublishing.com

Printed in the United States of America

Acknowledgments

So many people made this project a reality, and I'm so grateful.

It is a blessing to count George Jr. and Linda LeMaster as not only friends but valued ministry partners. It is my prayer, I've done your story proud and that by sharing it, others will find hope in hopelessness and find purpose with a life where Jesus Christ is in control. Thank you for sharing your story.

I'm grateful to the good staff at Christian Faith Publishing for helping with the many details of this book.

My wife Carla looked at early drafts and made good suggestions. Thank you for your support and encouragement.

Our children, Andrew, Shannon, and Andrew's wife, Julie, have also helped spur on this writing project.

Most of all, I'm grateful to Jesus Christ for salvation given to all, to me, and his help along the way, not only in the path of this book but in the whole path of life.

Dan Steinbeck

Introduction

George LeMaster had enough of his wretched life. His track record was less than stellar: a felony DWI arrest after wrecking his sister's car out of state, losing his license for three years, getting fired for trying to tell a boss how to run the business, trouble finding a job, the threat of losing his home, and perceived declining importance to family.

The above events and more included the common thread of alcohol. For two decades, alcohol had been the king of his life, ordering him to keep drinking. He had willingly complied, and it took a toll on him in virtually every way—socially, spiritually, physically, and relationally.

He had started with beer, then moved to whiskey, then vodka—the latter he mixed with the prescription drug valium. Two previous efforts at detoxification had failed. He needed his alcohol fix frequently to end the shakes brought on by the alcohol consumption.

George knew he was a miserable mess and decided to end his life. Feeling he was useless to his wife Linda and their three children, he took a .22 Magnum pistol with him and—mindful that he didn't want Linda to clean his mess—drove his pickup truck to the city dump about three miles from Wayland, Missouri. Thinking Linda could use the truck, he got out.

On this Valentine's Day in 1982, George got about ten feet away from the truck, sat in the cold where light snow covered the ground, put the gun to his head, cocked the hammer, and then…he saw the red in the snow.

Suddenly, nothing was ever the same.

Chapter 1

Growing Up in Wayland

Wayland, Missouri, is a simple, quiet, and private town and seems to have been for decades, perhaps as long as it has been in existence.

Some people have said modern Wayland is a place to go to get away from things, such as the law and bill collectors. Church officials have found they can visit an address one time and then several months later, go visit again and those occupants have left, and perhaps new ones are there, for the time being anyway.

That's not everyone, of course, who lives there. But there are a lot of the five hundred plus of the listed population who have lived there who don't make Wayland a permanent home.

The town was platted in 1880 and named for pioneer settler Jerre Wayland.

Like many other small towns around the globe, Wayland isn't home to a particularly known celebrity nor known for any major historical event.

Perhaps the closest fame for Wayland is the proximity to Athens, the site of Missouri's northernmost Civil War battle. Approximately fourteen miles separate the two towns as the crow flies. However, if the crow has to drive Missouri roads, it is closer to a twenty-two-and-a-half-mile drive.

Although George LeMaster Jr. has a story, he would be the first to say he's certainly no celebrity.

As Wayland is a simple town, George would say he's just a simple country boy from there.

George William LeMaster Jr. was born May 2, 1945, in Graham Hospital in Keokuk, Iowa [later Keokuk Area Hospital and in more recent years, part of the Blessing Healthcare System headquartered in Quincy, Illinois], a son of Mary Elizabeth "May Beth" Statler LeMaster and George Willis LeMaster Sr. George William was the oldest of seven children, followed by sisters Colleen, Connie, Carla, Martha, Jeri, and a brother Merle Wayne, the latter who died in infancy.

At his birth, World War II was beginning to end, and in the next few years, Wayland would thrive. George Jr. was a lifelong resident of this tiny town northeast of Missouri, except for that first year in Keokuk, Iowa, some thirteen miles east and north of Wayland.

"It was a simpler time. You obeyed your parents. You talked to your elders with 'Yes, ma'am. No, ma'am. Yes, sir. No, sir,'" he said.

Perhaps because World War II was in the past, the community was full of people with local and national pride, fully understanding respect for others and functioning well.

The turbulent '60s weren't there yet, and when they arrived, there was a different attitude in war and those who served. In both war cases, Wayland's war attitude reflected common feelings across the United States.

"[In the 1950s] We read the Bible in school. We had the American flag and the Christian flag in the classroom, and you said pledges of allegiance to both. Every Monday [in school], we were asked who went to church, and a chart was marked for those who went. Everything in Wayland seemed to revolve around the schools and the churches," George said.

George recalled Wayland being a *self-sufficient town* back then, with three or four grocery stores, a bowling alley, and a funeral home. There were three churches—Baptist, Catholic, and Methodist—and as George grimaced later, "And six taverns."

By contrast, in 2021, there was no grocery store, no funeral home, four churches [two Baptist, the Methodist, and a nondenominational cowboy church; St. Martha Catholic Church closed in 2018 and merged with St. Michael Catholic Church in Kahoka, Missouri], a truck stop with an attached Denny's, a convenience store, a newly opened truck mechanic business across Highway 136 from the truck stop, an ice cream shop, a laundromat, Reeds restaurant, a wholesale furnishings store, and a tattoo parlor which was popular among the locals.

Also gone by 2021 was the degree of self-sufficiency and the town's own school, having merged with several others into the Clark County R-1 School District in Kahoka decades earlier.

There always seems to be a place that sells alcohol in the town, and some locations of such sales may have changed through the years. In 2021, there were still several alcohol sales locations—some offering it in open drinks and some, like convenience stores, offering it in packaged containers.

"We were poor and didn't know because the government didn't tell us we were poor," he said.

Maybe once a month in the 1950s and 1960s, the LeMaster family would go to Kahoka, nine miles west, or to Keokuk, Iowa, shopping for items not locally purchased.

"Keokuk, especially at Christmastime, had all the stuff in the stores."

When he came of age, George Jr. did not serve in the military, but he tried. He was classified 1A in May 1964, classified 3A in May 1965, and classified 1Y in 1966. The last classification, 1Y, meant deferred due to medical conditions, those being him underweight, color-blind, and asthmatic.

"I had signed up at selective service at the post office. 1A meant ready to go. 3A was an only son provision. 1Y meant you were no longer eligible. Then Vietnam happened and there were draft dodgers to Canada. If you went to Vietnam and came home, you were treated like dirt. If you did not go, you were treated like dirt. If you were a draft dodger, it seems like you were treated well."

Decades later, and no longer eligible for anything in the military, George Jr. still carries his cards saying he had indeed signed up with selective service and was not accepted in.

"I was not a draft dodger, and I still carry my card in case someone thinks otherwise," he said.

In the hills of Wayland, actually closer to the northern border city of St. Francisville, Marysville—now a defunct footnote of Clark County, Missouri history—sat in the hollow. The trading post was just above St. Francisville.

A trading post was set up by William R. Harrison and Charles Wood of the American Fur Company of St. Louis. They set up the post in September 1882 after trading with Sac and Fox Indians, including Chief Blackhawk and Keokuk, but didn't return there for better than six years.

The town was named Marysville because five of the first settlers' wives were named Mary.[1] It grew from there for a while.

"At one time, it was a good-sized town of about 250 people. Saturday nights were parties.

"My great-grandfather Hiram Boatman [who died in 1894] lived with an Indian squaw in Marysville. He came home drunk one night. People said they could hear hollering like a wounded wolf. She had strung up my great-grandfather by his thumbs with his feet just off the ground. He couldn't use his thumbs after that, but he gave up drinking."

The tough squaw reportedly chewed hides to soften them.

The great-grandfather's activities showed an early presence of alcohol in the LeMaster's family line.

Marysville was also the birthplace of George Willis LeMaster Sr.

George Jr. has fond memories of growing up in Wayland.

"The church bells rang, and the churches were full. Wayland was a good little town. Everyone knew what everyone else was doing. You only got the newspaper to see who got caught.

"Kids in our neighborhood gravitated to our house. Mom had homemade bread for us. In our neighborhood, you could either find the kids at our house or Martha and Bill Coop's house across the street from us. Their daughter Cheryl was like a sixth sister to me, or my sisters and I would be over at the Coop's house.

---

[1] Marysville information is from a news article, date and publication not immediately known, written by Hazel LeMaster, a great aunt of George LeMaster Jr. It should not be confused with the current Missouri town Maryville.

"I'd also go to Ricky and Ronnie Roberts' house two doors down from Mom and Dad and play with them. Everybody knew where everybody was. We stayed within Mom's voice. When she called, we'd come back," he said.

George LeMaster Sr. worked at Morris Garage in Wayland as Junior was growing up. At times, George Sr. was town marshal, mayor, fire chief, and municipal judge but wasn't the fire chief and marshal at the same time.

May Beth LeMaster was a telephone operator in Wayland, working while her children were in school at the switchboard on Main Street in Wayland.

"We had the old crank telephones that were powered with two round one-and-a-half volt batteries that the phone company replaced every year. I would call Mom just to talk to her. She told me not to call unless it was an emergency.

"We had a party line, and our number was 33. When Mom tried to call out, she'd hear the click of other people picking up their lines. She knew who was listening in and told them to hang up [if it wasn't the party to whom she wanted to speak]. When Dad was fire chief and marshal, we got a private line, and his number was 36."

There was no other law enforcement in Wayland proper other than the town marshal.

"The marshal was more of a peace officer. If you needed the police, you called Charlie Milligan [Clark County, Missouri sheriff] who would come down from Kahoka. He was a good guy."

Once, when George Jr. was age thirteen or fourteen, Charlie Milligan found George at the Wayland City dump.

"I had driven a two-and-a-half ton 1929 Chevrolet truck and loaded with oil cans. Charlie found me there and asked if my father was around. I said, 'Yeah, somewhere.'"

Charlie Milligan was wise enough to know better.

"Charlie followed me back to town. He told Dad, 'George was driving again. I know George knows how to drive, and he's a good driver, but he can't drive the truck. However, if you put the oil cans in a trailer and haul it with a tractor, he could drive it all over town.'"

At that time, George Jr. was making "good money" for driving the truck, albeit illegally—ten cents an hour.

George Jr. recalled pumping gas at gravity-fed pumps at Morris Garage as well. He also cleaned parts by dipping them in gas so they could be put back together clean and swept the floors at the garage.

Public service continued in the LeMaster family in later years.

The elder LeMaster's daughter Colleen [South] has also served as Mayor in the 2000s. Connie [Handyside] has served as an emergency responder. Martha's husband Randy Ewart has been in law enforcement and both Martha and Randy, as well as their two daughters, have been in Southern Baptist Disaster Relief, as have been Connie and her late husband Richard. Jeri Bradley is a schoolteacher in Iowa. Carla (South) volunteered at the Sever-Clark County Library located in Kahoka and a food pantry in Kahoka before her passing.

"I typically hung around the garage where Dad worked. He was my idol.

"I grew up fast. The old-timers used to sit in front of the garage and talk about people. I'd hear things and repeat them. Mom would say, 'Where did you hear that?' and had to rein it in. Mom kept Dad in line. Dad was hardheaded. Mom was the grounding force.

"At home, Dad would turn down his hearing aids, and when Mom found out, she threatened to put them where the sun didn't shine," George recalled.

As a child, George Jr. attended Wayland Public School Number 45 through the eighth grade, then went for two years at Revere School before transferring to Kahoka for his final two years.

"This Wayland was my world. I didn't like the school at Kahoka. There was less hands-on teaching than there was at Revere.

"In high school at Revere, Mrs. Lula Downing, an English teacher, said we had to do oral book reports. I offered to do two written ones instead. She insisted on the oral report. She said, 'Mr. LeMaster'—she always called me that—'Mr. LeMaster, you never know when you will be speaking before others.'"

Despising the thought of public speaking, and although denying such a need would arise, her words would be revisited later in George LeMaster Jr.'s life.

He took a year of elementary electronics at Keokuk Community College after graduating from high school.

In his youth, George and his friends and sisters became acquainted with the Wayland City dump, about three miles northeast of Wayland on a gravel road. They would go there to retrieve items thrown away and rebuild or repurpose them, fishing them out from among the tin cans, bottle glass shards, and food scraps.

"We called the dump City Supply."

Young enterprising people enjoyed searching for prizes among the garbage. The adage, "one man's trash is another one's treasure," was at play here.

At City Supply, bicycle parts, lawn mower decks, old fans, and anything that could be recycled for the finder's own use or to fix and resell for spending money was scavenged and brought back into town or saved for their own use or at times given away.

George Jr. called himself a repairer. For example, discarded box fans were brought home from City Supply. George would disassemble them, relubricate or replace ball bearings, reassemble them, and give the now working fans away.

It seems George Jr. always had a knack for mechanical work, a family trait that extended through several generations.

"My grandpa, Robert John LeMaster, could fix anything. My Dad had the mechanical ability, and that's what he taught me. For cars, Dad had certain rules I follow even today—change the oil and keep the engine clean."

George Sr. was also a scavenger/inventor of types. It's not known if he also went to City Supply, but he, too, came home with objects found.

In a case of inventorship gone awry, George Sr. brought a broken airplane propeller from the Kahoka Municipal Airport and put a two-speed electric motor on it at home.

"It sucked too much air and put Mom's new curtains in the neighbor's yards. It worked, but it was too much of a draw for that size window," George Jr. recalled with a laugh.

Music was an important component of the LeMaster home.

"A granddad I never met [Robert John] died in 1940, but he was self-taught on a violin.

"My uncle, Walter Lee LeMaster, was a local radio and TV star. He was known as Sagebrush Sandy. He was sponsored by Tri-State Dairy. His lead guitarist was Don Johnson [one of those with whom George later played in bar bands]."

Sagebrush was a nickname from a childhood haircut, and Sandy referred to the hair's color. He did a live half-hour afternoon children's program first on KOKX radio in Keokuk, then on WGEM television located in Quincy, Illinois in the 1950s. His horse was named Flash. The shows were filmed in an upstairs studio, and it apparently was always an experience getting Flash on the elevator.

Sagebrush and his Serenaders cut several records in a Nashville studio. A master copy was brought to Carthage, Illinois, and pressed into vinyl products. Don Johnson was a guitarist with the Serenaders.[2]

"Dad played guitar a little until he broke two fingers honing down a cylinder on a six-cylinder car [at Morris Garage]. It caught on the crankshaft and busted two fingers. He taped the fingers together but never went to a doctor. It ended his guitar playing.

"Uncle John, Dad's oldest brother [of six siblings], played bass guitar with the family at reunions and visits. Martha and Connie would play the piano. All the sisters except Carla sung."

A late 1960s auto accident near Memphis, Missouri left Carla with a monotone voice, George later explained.

Still, the LeMasters often had country music or gospel music that was played and/or sang in the home.

"Each country song had a message. After I was saved, I saw each gospel song had a sermon," George Jr. said.

He got his first guitar in 1964 and taught himself how to play it "with [eventual wife] Linda's patience."

"Mom and Dad took us to the Methodist Church in Wayland. Mom would say, 'The kids were going to Sunday school.' Dad said

---

[2] Information on Sagebrush Sandy came from a 2014 Bonny Buyer (shopper) news article.

he had a headache. Mom said to take care of it at church, or Dad said he couldn't get up Sunday morning. Mom said, 'You will.'

"I was in church and Sunday school most of my life [to that point]. We were the janitors of the Methodist Church. Rev. Hollis Wilhelm was there. When Rev. Wilhelm left, the Wayland Methodist Church became affiliated with the United Methodist branch.

"Mom's grandfather was a Presbyterian minister. Mom's dad abandoned Mom and my grandma.

"Mom's family was dysfunctional. Her father left her and Mom's mother when she was young. It didn't really affect me then because I didn't know what a Presbyterian was, but his son left. Grandma and Mom didn't talk about why he left, and I never heard why. Around here, if a man leaves his family, he's as worthless as a three-dollar bill."

George recalled once his mother, curious to fill in missing blanks of her past, tracked her father to Washington State, and she went out to see him.

"She was not well received by his family [out west]. She came back with more questions than answers.

"One day as we were cleaning the church, I was dusting the pulpit. I turned on the public address system. I always loved playing with electronics. I was singing into the microphone. I didn't know the sound went downstairs where Mom was.

"Mom was always what I would call religious even when we didn't go to church. Mom came up and told me, 'Say, you look good behind the pulpit.'

"I said, 'I don't think so.' I had seen preachers put on pedestals," George said.

George LeMaster Jr. was disillusioned by the ministry.

"What I had seen from the Methodist Church was they would make pastors move on. There was one pastor who had three boys, and they were boys. We [my friends and I] always welcomed the new kids to the community.

"But someone would complain about the boys' actions, or the wife was wearing the wrong type of clothes to church [according to the other women of the church]. I've always thought you are who you are and that don't change because of your clothes. God looks here [he said, patting his heart].

"And Grandpa was a Presbyterian preacher whose son left his wife. And there were fake preachers on TV. I didn't hold preachers in too high esteem. I didn't want to have anything to do with it [ministry]."

Despite obvious turnoffs to the prospect of being a minister, the words spoken by his mother early in his life would find an eventual fit with an unsuspecting George Jr.

"Mom and Dad pulled out of the Methodist Church after pastor Rev. Wilhelm left. We had Bible studies with Mom and Dad. I read the Bible, but I'm not sure it did any good at that point. Mom was the anchor in the home like you were, Linda, when I was boozing," George would say decades later to his wife.

Spiritually, what he was hearing at church and at home didn't take root in George Jr.'s heart.

Chapter 2

Love Blossoms

Linda South, a year younger than George Jr., lived in Keokuk, Iowa for the first eighteen or so years of her life. Her parents were Helen Anna Johnson South and Victor Milton South.

She was the baby of the family. Her family included sister Delores Lambert and brothers Jerry South, Larry South [who married Colleen LeMaster], and Chester South [who married Carla LeMaster]. Only Linda and Chester are left of the South family in 2021. The other siblings have passed on.

"I always wanted to go to church as a child but was not able to go. Mom raised herself and her siblings. Her mom died when she was eight years old, and her dad died when she was eighteen. She was poor and unable to get to church. My parents both later told me they were saved," Linda said, grateful for the hope.

"My paternal grandma was a strict Christian, but her Christianity was not loving. It was rules. My grandma and grandpa never had a lot to do with us. We were on the outs as a family. My dad used to go, but one time [as a youth], he played baseball and came to church dirty. He and his friends got there late, and they [church] asked him to leave because he wasn't dressed right. Plus, he took so much from grandma being so strict.

"Dad later drank, so we didn't go to church," Linda said. "His drinking took household money needed for family finances."

Unfortunately, Linda would later relive how someone else's drinking would affect family finances.

Linda's father stopped drinking in the 1950s when her mother *laid down the law.*

"One lady took me to church on Christmas and Easter. The other kids thought I was only there for the candy. One time, when I was seven or eight, I was given a Bible, and I was so happy. I took it home and played church," Linda said.

"I loved Sunday school, but the kids weren't really friendly to me because I didn't come all the time.

"I read the Bible. It meant a lot to me, but I didn't understand it. Maybe I sang a song," she said, recalling her time at home *playing church* of the few services she had seen.

Linda LeMaster noted that the church had great respect for the Word of God and didn't want anything put on top of a Bible, not even a piece of paper.

"I had a friend that lived behind another church and met her parents. He was a pastor. He asked if I knew Jesus. I didn't know. He asked if I wanted to be saved, and I prayed the sinner's prayer, but I didn't know [at that time] what I was doing, but I felt that God had me then," Linda said.

She was about nine years old at the time.

"When I first met George, his family would go to church. I didn't. It was through his family I was introduced to church. I came down on weekends [from Keokuk] and went to church with his family," Linda said.

"Connie always loved the Lord and was a good influence on my life. It was at a youth meeting about the Rapture when I gave my heart to the Lord at age nineteen. I don't remember stepping out. I just remember being down there [at the front of the service]."

The irony of which of the couple was in church and who wasn't would play out years later. Already, the one frequently in church at that time wasn't as fond of church as the one who longed to be there and couldn't.

The couple dated from 1962 to 1965. They were drawn together by common interests of picnicking, camping, and the outdoors.

"And she was cute. Still is," George said many years later.

The church changed affiliations after that, and it was sometime later Linda was baptized after her marrying George. Decades later, she was baptized into the Freedom in Christ Church in Kahoka, Missouri.

George was by her in the pew when Linda accepted Jesus into her heart, but he did not choose to respond then to the call to come to Christ.

"I had a tight hold of the pew. I fought going forward," George said of his decision not to follow Linda, or at that time, Christ.

"God had prepared me ahead of time for what I was [about to be] going through. If I hadn't met him, I wouldn't be where I was either," Linda said.

The *him* to whom Linda referred to was George because through his family and being with him, Linda became a Christian. But the *him* she mentioned could have just as easily been said about Jesus Christ, who has long been an important part of her life.

Where Linda had the first acceptance of Christ, it wasn't as easy for George, and it didn't materialize until much later.

"I knew about Jesus, but I didn't know him personally," George said.

Linda recalls when Rev. Wilhelm preached, he had tears streaming down his cheeks.

George and Linda married shortly after the Youth for Christ event in the Wayland Methodist Church in June 1965 when he was twenty and she was nineteen. They made their home in Wayland.

"People said our marriage wouldn't last because we were too young," George said.

Several years later, the family grew and eventually included children Mary, born in 1967; George Victor III, born in 1969; and Robert, born in 1971.

"Linda had the kids at the Baptist Church in Wayland when there was only one Baptist church. I was hit-and-miss [in attendance]," George said.

After leaving the Methodist Church, George's family went to the Baptist Church in Wayland.

"When two or three of the LeMasters left the Methodist Church, the whole LeMaster clan did too," George said.

Linda worked at Shelor Globe, a rubber manufacturing plant in Keokuk, and she retired as a machine operator after thirty years with the company that included multiple tasks.

She also worked as a domestic house cleaner, cleaning other people's homes while her kids were in school.

Linda's father died in 1986, and her mother died in 1994.

Chapter 3

The Growing Presence of Alcohol

George LeMaster Jr. had an early introduction to alcohol. He was first exposed to alcohol when he was maybe twelve years old at his home.

"Mom was of German descent and did not drink. Dad drank beer and made beer. He also drank whiskey," George said.

"When Dad worked at the garage, there were several people in town who made beer. You could make sixty quarts for yourself without paying taxes. Now there were some guys in the rural parts of Wayland who were making moonshine, but no one was to know about that.

(Moonshine was whiskey made illegally, in part because no taxes were paid on its manufacture.)

"Dad began to make beer. When he first started, it was not bad-tasting beer. The more he experimented, he got in trouble."

There were a lot of on-the-street stories and theories about how to improve the beer's flavor. George Sr. apparently fell for several ideas, with most becoming abysmal failures. The younger George was around age thirteen or fourteen at the time when the beer-brewing experimentation began.

Once, George Sr. bought a huge cream separator. He tried using it in brew production, with the theory being removing the yeast supposedly would make better-tasting beer.

"Beer foams, milk doesn't. The beer was supposed to run out of one side of the separator like the milk did, but all it did was run over the back porch and soaked into the old wooden porch floor. When it got hot outside, the porch smelled of stale beer."

Another theory the senior LeMaster also tried was putting raisins in the brewed product to remove the yeast. They swelled the raisins "as big as plums and blew up," George Jr. recalled of his father's efforts.

Then George Sr. had a hydrometer, a tapered glass tube with a weight dropped in it as the beer gets worked.

"When it got to the red line, the beer was ready to be bottled. If the needle goes below the line, the beer goes flat. If it gets above the red line, it builds up power and takes out Mom's canning."

George Sr. had hurried one brewing project because of some other appointment, and the unfinished beer product was put in the basement with the intent to bottle it later. The brewed product was still above the red line.

"The beer was put in the cellar green. Suddenly, we heard explosions and glass crashing. It blew all sixty quarts of beer up and broke 90 percent of Mom's canned tomatoes, peaches, and beans and sent glass shards into the basement ceiling [among other places] below George Jr.'s room. Mom said, 'Well, clean it up.'"

Amazingly, Mary LeMaster let George Sr. live.

Eventually, the elder LeMaster determined buying beer was easier than making it himself.

"The reason I drank was I liked the taste of beer. I don't remember getting a buzz from it because I ate when I was drinking. I first started having trouble at age twenty-one. I was free, white, and twenty-one," George Jr. said.

"I started running around with my cousin Stanley LeMaster, about 1967, who played guitar with Don Johnson. Don played lead guitar. I did the singing. We played in different *clubs*, we called them. They were dives."

"Donnie, Stanley, and I went in there and drank and partied all Saturday nights. Sunday mornings I had a head full of hurt.

"I learned why there is chicken wire in some bars. It keeps the [thrown] bottles from hitting you as you played. I said, 'If they had chicken wire, I wasn't going to sing.' It was not only the bottles, but the beer would still get all over you."

Obviously, the liquid would not be contained by chicken wire as glass bottles would be.

"I'd play songs, and there'd be some guy crying, three sheets to the wind, and he kept drinking. We'd play songs that played on his emotions, so the guy would keep drinking. That still bothers me," George said years later of the new realization when the Holy Spirit changes a perspective.

He said some bars offered kickbacks to the bands in cash or free drinks if they got others to drink. Getting a three-sheets-to-the-wind sad sack to cry would mean he'd buy another beer to drown out his miseries, and maybe buy a round for others gathered. Bars liked having this type of patron.

"Some of the bar patrons would buy the band a beer, and there would be three or four beers there to drink. I'd drink some on the break. I'd have to stay sober or blow it."

But George found it difficult to drink even some of the beers and still stay sober. He tried to focus on his bar singing with varying degrees of success.

He reflected later on, discovering the difference in country-and-western and beer-joint songs.

"Beer joint songs were about drinking and cheating and everything that goes against God's word. I never had any satisfaction playing at the bars," he said.

Still, despite reporting no satisfaction playing the bar circuit, he kept doing so.

George knew the alcohol was his own growing problem, too, but he found a strange loop of the situation. He seemed to drink to get away from the problem. The problem was his drinking.

Lyrics from a theatrical production explained the mindset of George as he drank, playing in bars and not enjoying it: "*Have another drink when you think that the drink that you drunk isn't doing enough for you.*"

"My drinking started to get bad when I was at work at Thomas Truck [a dolly cart manufacturer] in Keokuk. Previously, I worked at Western Auto from 1963 to 1968. I graduated from weekend drunk to full-time drinker."

His family began to clue into his alcohol problem in 1970 when he was physically sick, losing weight, and missing work.

"Mom, Dad, and Linda all talked to me about going downhill health-wise. I couldn't remember things like about our last son. They told me they were concerned and that I needed help," he said.

"Linda was going in surgery, and I went out to get some flowers for her and also get some alcohol. I had enough alcohol in me. I almost passed out. I don't remember a lot of raising Robert. This was the time I started to have problems with my memory."

Although George was aware of his problem, and his family was, too, it wasn't in George's makeup to actively pursue nonalcoholic choices.

He worked at Thomas from 1968 to 1979 before an inglorious departure, telling the boss how to run his business. It should go without saying George, a regular alcoholic, was not in any position to make company leadership decisions.

"I'd drink a can of stale beer before going to work. I was drinking whiskey too. I carried a bottle with me to work. It got bad enough that every fifteen minutes I needed a drink, or I got the shakes."

In 1971, George wrecked his sister Connie's car in Iowa. There was damage to the left front fender of Connie's Chevrolet. He was arrested and charged with driving while intoxicated and a felony over $500 when the accident broke the front end off of an aftermarket fiberglass unibody-constructed Ford of the other car owner, thereby totaling the unibody car.

"I was in over my head."

Family bailed him out, but because Missouri has a reciprocal agreement on DWI arrests with Iowa, George lost his driver's license for three years.

Fellow Wayland residents Bob Butcher and Donnie Toops then gave George rides to work at Thomas for three years until he got his license back.

"I still didn't learn my lesson. After I got my license back, I continued to drink and drive. Brilliant," a wiser George said in self-disgust decades later.

He never had another accident but had other alcohol problems.

"The havoc the alcohol wreaked was on my health and on my family. I was giving a lot of verbal and mental abuse. Linda had grounds for divorce many times over."

His alcoholism grew worse.

"In my drinking days, I chased the neon rainbow and lived the honky-tonk dream. You'd hear 'You can make it big.' That was a lie of Satan. The devil said I was having a good time."

Even though at times he was miserable, George bought into Satan's "good time" lies. Still, George had a realistic look at where his level of music understanding was relative to the pipe dreams of a Nashville career. Satan's lies were somewhat enticing.

George developed those opinions of Nashville from Sagebrush, who recorded his work in Nashville and brought home the master copy to be produced at a Carthage, Illinois radio station. George's cousin Stanley LeMaster went to Nashville intent on cutting a record, too, and came back after two days, realizing to make it in Nashville, people need an inside track and the *go-for-it spirit* to work at making it big.

The Baptist church where George and Linda attended decided to help George.

"In the early 1970s, the Wayland Baptist Church sent me to Thomas Road Baptist Church in Lynchburg, Virginia for their home for alcoholics to dry me out. It was Jerry Falwell's church. I went for thirty days.

"They monitored my vitals, but they gave me no medical intervention. They wanted you to read the Bible and get you into church. They put us in a gallery. When the TV cameras went out, Jerry [Falwell] pointed us out to the audience. We were a tool he used.

"When they took the offerings in that church, there were *clunk, clunk* sounds. The doors automatically locked during the offering.

"We were bused to the church, going by Falwell's house. It was an estate. It was walled and had watchtowers on the corners. I called them gun turrets. We alcoholics on the bus called it *Jerry's Prison*."

This was a spiritual effort of sorts of Falwell to get alcoholics to sober up, but driving by the mansion made the alcoholics in the program question his true motives. It isn't immediately known the success for other alcoholics in Falwell's treatment programs, but for the Wayland, Missouri resident, it was not impressive enough to give up the hooch.

While in Virginia, Linda and the kids scoured the house for hidden alcohol and found multiple containers, which were all dumped out. For example, a pair of boots each concealed some alcohol.

"I thought I only hid one or two bottles," George said. Linda looked at George incredulously when he said that decades later because what was found was certainly more than two containers.

When he got out of the detoxification effort in Virginia, George answered Satan's call to continue boozing it up.

When it was learned George was back to his drinking ways, a Wayland Baptist church member told Linda, "George had let the church down" and proclaimed, "George will never stop drinking."

Linda, who had been seeking her own consolation in George's situation, was hurt by those words; first being told the church was offended, and then the seemingly hopeless declaration.

"Still, there were a lot of nice people who stood by us. When George was in Lynchburg, Virginia trying to dry out, Gene Baker, [later a Hamilton, Illinois, pastor] took the LeMaster children to McDonald's, and his wife Margaret took Linda shopping.

"She bought me scented stationery so I could write to George. The kids had never got to eat out before the Bakers took them. The Bakers also paid a gas bill and paid when I needed new glasses," Linda said.

"I came back and started drinking again. I was right back where I started, and it got worse."

Two years later, George went through another detoxification effort at Keokuk Area Hospital.

"Dr. John Vance, a private practice chiropractor in Keokuk, Iowa, said there was nothing he could do for me, and took me to the hospital. I had the shakes if I didn't get alcohol. They brought me out of it medically," he said.

In 1972, to help George with the shakes from the delirium tremens [DTs], he was prescribed valium.

"One counselor said I drank 'because my wife drove me to drink, and I didn't like my mother.' I told him he was full of it. My wife didn't drive me to do anything, and I loved my mother. I told him I was a mess, and I liked to drink. *I* was the one that got in over my head, and it was *my* fault I was in this situation.

"At night, I was sweating, and it turned the sheets yellow and created an odor."

The alcohol seemed like an insurmountable problem, and it had a strong pull on George, as it does with other alcoholics.

While still a drinker, George did attend a revival service at Wayland Baptist with Linda. After the service, George—perhaps under some conviction—made a beeline outside and smoked a cigarette.

"One pastor at the revival told George, even when he was still drinking, 'God has a plan for you,'" Linda recalled.

Linda said even as she taught Sunday school and vacation Bible school, George helped her make projects for those classes.

The Wayland Baptist pastor talked to Farmers Home Administration, a federal housing agency, and the LeMasters got to keep their house at 311 West Des Moines Street in Wayland.

"I did pretty good the first couple of years (at Thomas Truck). I was in maintenance, a machinist, and when someone didn't show up for work, I was a spray painter.

"Harry Miller was a preacher who worked in the office of Thomas Truck. He witnessed to me [about the Lord]. He prayed. He helped us financially. He ran interference between me and the boss. He did all that was humanly possible to share Jesus, and I'd have none of it."

Also trying to witness to George at Thomas Truck was fellow employee Donnie Gillpin, who was finding the efforts the same way Harry was—frustrating.

"Still, I was under the influence. No, the alcohol influenced my life. Harry Miller saw me duck into the tavern across the alley from Thomas during work," George said, adding he had a way he could get in and help himself to drinks, even while he was at work.

"That's when I hit the skids, and that's when I knew I had a problem. I was a cheap drunk. I took valium and vodka. It would wind me up quick, but it didn't last, and the longer I went, the shorter [each cycle] lasted," George said.

"The doctor said he was trying to bring my nerves back to normal. I didn't know where I was. The doctor said I was a functioning alcoholic.

"Each time I was released from these programs, I would return to the *old ways* and each time alcoholism would progress another step."

Harry, the pastor/coworker at Thomas Truck, came to visit George at his home.

"Once, Harry told me he wanted me to help him look at a car. I thought he doesn't need me for that. Harry was trying to keep me out of a beer joint. He admitted that later.

"Harry was instrumental in praying for me and witnessing, and he would be at my house. He said, 'The Lord told me to come and see you.' I was sitting there drinking a can of beer. As he talked, I crushed the beer can in my hands."

"The devil didn't want you to hear that," Linda offered of George's response.

Chapter 4

A Matter of Desperation, a Moment of Truth

Things were just not going well for George, and it was because he had put himself and his family in this predicament. He knew he was the problem. He just didn't know the solution.

Three years had passed since the second unsuccessful effort to detoxify George LeMaster Jr.

"Through my stupor, I could see my life, my family, my home, and my job slipping from me because I could not stop it. My life was completely out of control because of alcohol and drugs.

"I lost my job of ten years as a machinist. In 1979, we nearly lost our home, and because of verbal and mental abuse, was well on the way to losing my wife and three children."

After being fired at Thomas Truck in 1979 for trying to tell the boss how to run his company, later that year he took a security job through Wackenhut Security. George later called it *rent-a-cop*.

He was assigned to Shelor Globe, an automotive parts manufacturer in Keokuk, Iowa.

One night, there were thieves outside of Shelor Globe stealing obsolete aluminum molds.

"Our supervisor sent me and the other security officer out back in the boondocks. My partner and I went around different sides. As he came around a corner, it was cold and a full moon was shining on his badge. I thought if his badge shines, so does mine. It reflected [light] as a mirror."

Realizing this exposed him as security, possibly increasing the risk to his safety, he quit that job in the coming month, ending his security guard duty after a year and a half.

"If you did your job, it was wrong, and if you didn't, it was wrong. You would put things in a write-up and give it to a supervisor, and nothing would get done and it would come back on you."

After being a security guard, George was hired by Lester Piersee to repair Kirby vacuums. He was still drinking at the time.

The alcoholism continued, further eroding his family relationships.

"I could see how I was hurting Linda. At the time, I was drinking vodka and taking valium."

George falsely proclaimed the vodka was odorless, perhaps trying to convince himself. Said Linda, "I could smell it."

George gave a lot of thought about City Supply, better known as the Wayland dump. He knew the way, having gone there for years to bring home items that had been thrown away to give them a new life.

It [the city dump] was a place for discarded things, George thought, feeling discarded himself from society, and by his own doing, all but discarded by family.

One Sunday morning in February 1982—on Valentine's Day, no less—George saw his hopelessness mushroom and decided hope was gone. He would end his life.

"I was sitting in the house. Linda was out with the kids, taking them to church. I was living on vodka and valium. We were about to lose our house. I think I weighed ninety-six pounds at the time. I sat at the kitchen table. I felt I might as well end it all. I was no use to anyone."

The term *living* might be an exaggeration. George LeMaster Jr. was existing and barely doing that.

"I didn't want to do this [suicide] in the house when Linda would have to clean it up. I did think about Linda and the kids. I was losing my mind. I loved them [Linda and the kids] dearly, but I needed alcohol more."

George knew what happens when one takes a life, having seen the remains of some from Wayland who did so. Those images weren't enough to persuade him not to consider doing this.

Sometime before this, Linda asked George, "If you had to choose between me or the bottle, what would you choose?"

To George, the choice was easy. "The bottle."

"As I remember, I was sick and tired of waking up sick and tired. All I had seen was to drink to hit a plateau, but I had been to the point I didn't care anymore. I wasn't drinking for a buzz. There was no buzz toward the end. It kept me going."

The bottle he despised was ironically his choice for perpetual comfort which didn't last. It was time, in George's mind, to put a stop to the madness.

George grabbed his Ruger .22 Magnum revolver and some critical-defense hollow-point .45 grain bullets.

He had taken a gun to the dump before to shoot rats that he said were "as big as house cats."

"We kept our aim good by popping them," George said.

Otherwise, the guns in the LeMaster house were mainly used for hunting food or were collector guns including a .22 semiautomatic squirrel rifle, a 16-gauge shotgun, a 30-30 deer rifle, a 6.5-millimeter Japanese military rifle, and a .308 German Mauser.

This Valentine's Day, 1982, George had a different reason for taking the revolver to the dump.

"I went to the dump outside of town where all useless things end up and prepared to take my life. It was about ten or eleven o'clock in the morning. There was a cove there at the dump. It was big enough to pull a pickup truck into it, and no one could easily see it."

He didn't write out a suicide note, actually ashamed of where alcohol had brought him.

"I got out. I didn't want to do it in the truck because I thought Linda could use the truck. I got about ten feet from the truck and sat in the light, wet snow. I was thinking, *I'll catch a cold*, but then I thought, *It won't make a difference because I'll be dead*."

February winters in northeast Missouri are brutal, and winds are raw. So it was on this day in 1982. The temperature at this time was at freezing or slightly over, and the wind was twelve to twenty miles per hour, enough to make being outside a cold experience. George was ill-equipped for the weather, wearing blue jeans, a pull-over sweatshirt, a cap, and a light jacket.

"I was going to put the pistol in my mouth, then I put the pistol to my temple and cocked the hammer."

Nanoseconds from a decision where he would have entered eternity without God, something else happened.

"I looked to my right and saw a red dot in the snow. I laid down the cocked gun and set it in the snow. Everything but the red dot was covered with a skiff of snow. I picked it up and brushed the snow off of it. It was facedown, all wet, and very prominent."

Curiosity of what was semiburied in the snow changed George's focus. He was used to having things catch his eye when the dump was his City Supply.

The *red dot* was a part of the cover of a Gideon's International pocket New Testament given at that time to some unknown child and later discarded, with the reason of its discarding also unknown.

Unfortunately, not everyone values having a Bible. In fairness, the discarded Bible may have just been an extra one a family had, and there was no idea of another way to dispose of it.

Whether the child or someone else highlighted some scriptures on the open, facedown pages were also part of the mystery. On the pages still attached beneath that testament cover, three verses of a passage were underlined in red pencil. Still, the New Testament, although at one time belonging to a child, was discarded.

What was unimportant to someone to be thrown away became lifesaving, life-giving, and life-changing to George LeMaster Jr.

"That was God's last call [to pull me from alcoholism], sitting in the snow," George said.

George picked up the New Testament, swollen from being in the wet snow, facedown. He turned it over and saw three verses from James chapter 4—verses 7, 8, and 10—were underlined.

Those verses say in the King James Version:

*Submit yourselves therefore to God. Resist the devil,
and he will flee from you. Draw nigh to God, and
he will draw nigh to you. Cleanse your hands, ye
sinners; and purify your hearts, ye double minded.
[Be afflicted, and mourn, and weep: let your laugh-
ter be turned to mourning, and your joy to heavi-
ness] Humble yourselves in the sight of the Lord, and
he shall lift you up.*

Verse 9, which wasn't underlined, is in parenthesis above.

"Something clicked in my mind. I picked up the gun and went home," he said, adding he took the Bible home with him.

He left the Wayland City dump after an unknown amount of time had passed.

What clicked with George wasn't the trigger or the hammer but an intangible presence of God figuratively speaking at a moment critical to George's alcohol-damaged brain. Somewhere hidden in the memories, there was a holy reminder of this God, the subject of sermons and hymns of church services and Bible studies years earlier, who was still around and active.

Ironically, City Supply had given him something intrinsically more valuable than bike parts or lawn mower pieces brought home before. Where George gave new life to some items in the past, now it was time for George to get a new life himself.

"I came home from the dump, put the gun away, and laid the Bible downstairs in the workshop because it was wet. I came upstairs and changed. When you are cold and wet for a while, you start itching from the cold. That's why I changed clothes. I was ready to lay down and die," George said.

No one else knew at this time what George planned to do that day. Apparently, no one else was at the dump at that time either. After getting home, the thought of death still occurred to George but just not by suicide. He just figured he wasn't well enough to live.

"The next day you had your seizure," Linda said.

33

An ambulance was called and took George to Keokuk (Iowa) Area Hospital, where a Dr. Kemp treated him, calling George's condition *severe*. In the hospital, George had another seizure.

It is an understatement to say things didn't look well for George.

"I caught pneumonia and wound up in the hospital. This was my third time to dry out. I had consumed vodka and valium and moonshine from the hills of Wayland. I had pneumonia, and I had the DTs. I was a smoker. My immune system was shot."

[Delirium tremens—DTs—bring shaking, confusion, and hallucinations in an alcohol withdrawal and can be fatal.]

"The doctor said, 'You are still here? When you came in, you were turning gray, and I didn't think you'd make it through the night. Your heart was only beating when it felt like it.'"

George said it was the same doctor who had treated him on his second detoxification.

George developed pneumonia likely while sitting in the snow and wind without extra warm clothing or protection at the city dump. He was supposed to be dead now, and while he may have felt like it, he was breathing and talking, and not fully realizing he was being changed.

During his third dry-out time, Linda recalls George sitting up in bed once at the hospital and acting like he was rowing a boat. George had no memory of this, and he later admitted there are several years and many events during his alcoholic years where memory details are scarce.

"This bothers me. This black hole of my memory."

As one example later in George's recovery, Linda was going through some items to determine what to pitch and what to keep. She found a second-place ribbon George and former fellow tavern band partner Richard Patton had won in a talent show at the Kahoka School.

"I didn't remember playing at the school or winning the ribbon. I had vowed never to go back to the Kahoka school [after graduation]," he said.

People may forget things of the past, but George's alcoholism erased a lot of memories, some of which have never returned. In addition to forgotten memories, good and bad, alcoholic hallucinations were strong for George.

"There was a good-looking guy that pushed me in a tub," George said of the mind tricks.

Linda recalled there were times at home before this time George considered suicide where George saw *chewing gremlins* walking on the ceiling.

"He had the gun [holster] draped on the post of the bed. He wanted to shoot the gremlins. I said 'George, you can't see them.' They are from the devil. God protected me from the gun. I wanted to get George to understand you don't kill them with a gun but with the Word [of God]," Linda said.

"They [hallucinations] were real to me," he said.

However, he never actually tried to shoot the chewing gremlins, only suggesting he could do so.

"I woke up every morning and was sick and tired. In the hospital, it got me sobered up. At the end of the DTs, the muscles tensed then relaxed.

"A little grandma nurse in her sixties or seventies came in. She had a white dress and white hair. She had the kindest face but was [verbally] rough as a cob. I told her, 'I feel rugged. I feel like I got hit by a truck.' She said, 'You should. This is your third time, and if you come back here, I'll kick your [backside].'"

"I was indignant at her response. I told another nurse about her and that nurse didn't know about the grandma nurse. I talked to a doctor, and he went and checked into it. The doctor came back, and he said there was no one matching that description who worked that floor or in that hospital."

George wonders if "Grandma Nurse" might have been an angel, since no one else seemed to know about her, but the use of an inappropriate word bothered him. Someone told him it may have been the only way to get George's attention at that moment.

Still, it is a curious thing. If she was an angel, why was an inappropriate word used? If she wasn't an angel, why did no one on the hospital staff acknowledge her existence?

"God knew where I was," George said.

35

Chapter 5

Coached and Prayed into Sobriety

"I was trying to figure out how to put in action what I read in the Bible. I had to submit to God [verse 7], resist the devil [verse 7], draw near to God [verse 8], and humble myself in the sight of the Lord [verse 10], *then* he shall lift you up," George would later say in talks given about his testimony.

George had some friends who were ready to help him. Harry Miller, the one who had seen George sneak out of work at Thomas Truck and was pastor of the nondenominational Four Square Church in the powder town section of Keokuk (where gunpowder was once made), was one who helped George. Lester Piersee was another.

Lester, who attended a different church than Harry, had hired George at his Kirby vacuum cleaner shop in Keokuk when George was still drinking and remarked, "George can't walk and talk, but he could tear something apart and put it back together. I could guarantee what George fixed for a year. His work is impeccable, but he couldn't say two words."

George had learned the reassembly of items from his father and others in the LeMaster family line but practiced it as a youth washing vehicle parts in gasoline before reassembling them, and from fixing City Supply finds.

"Lester picked me up from the hospital. He got us groceries. We went to his house. In the den of his house is where it all took place. Lester said, 'You can be free of this [alcoholism].'"

At long last, George LeMaster Jr. was ready. They prayed, and George gave his heart to Jesus Christ.

"From that day on, I felt a weight was lifted. I was happy and wanted to tell everyone about Jesus. Drunks don't want to hear it," he said.

Gone instantly was George's desire and decades-old love for alcohol. Healed instantly was George's broken and alcohol-diseased body, except for lingering pneumonia symptoms.

"Mom always said she knew I'd quit drinking."

"The day Dr. Kemp released me, he gave me a checkup and manually found my liver was hard. About two weeks later, he checked my liver and said it was *normal*.

"He pushed my abdomen, looking for my liver problems. There was no pain when the doctor pushed. He said, 'You had cirrhosis of the liver, and now you don't.'"

I praised the Lord for my healing, and the doctor said, 'It had to be him [the Lord].'"

Yet it took more than two months for George to fully regain his strength from pneumonia.

"Harry Miller stuck with me the whole time. He said, 'I'm praying for you, and my church in Keokuk is praying for you.' Harry was instrumental in my support. You could see tears in his eyes when he talked to me," George said.

While true friends like Lester Piersee and Harry Miller were there for George, others in Wayland and the surrounding Missouri and Iowa communities who knew George's history of alcohol carried a more cynical attitude. "We'll see how long until he falls off the wagon."

Certainly, there was cause to be unconvinced of any change. Two previous detoxification efforts had failed. George LeMaster Jr. had a long history as a drunk, and many in Wayland knew it. This third dry-out effort would determine if history would repeat itself; would it be enough to end his life, or was this indeed a turning point in George LeMaster Jr.'s life?

Harry invited George and Linda to his church.

"I said, 'You don't want me in your church. I'm a drunk.' Harry said, 'You aren't anymore.'"

George took care of some small church tasks Harry gave him—collecting the Sunday school money to take to the church treasurer and ringing the bell to tell when Sunday school was over.

"Then he bought me a light blue leisure suit three or four weeks later."

[Leisure suits were made of polyester and were popular in the 1970s and early 1980s for men and often were cheaper than other suits.]

"When we went to Harry's church, it was very special, and the Spirit was there," Linda said.

George LeMaster Sr. also had given up drinking but did so a few years before George Jr. did.

When George Sr. quit drinking, years after giving up brewing his own, he took an order of unopened beer to Bobby Land of Alexandria, six miles east of Wayland in the store from where he had originally purchased it.

"Dad said the Lord spoke to him at Steel Castings [in Keokuk, Iowa where he worked] saying 'George, it's time to quit drinking.'"

George Sr. worked at Steel Castings for eighteen years between times at the Morris Garage and later the St. Francisville Toll Bridge.

Land saw the beer was unopened and bought the beer back, some twenty cases worth.

"Bobby thought the world was ending if George LeMaster Sr. was returning unopened beer. Dad tried to witness to me about the Bible and tell me what was in it after he gave up drinking," George Jr. said.

Perhaps it was a father's way to get the son to realize alcohol wasn't necessary for his life, wanting him to quit too.

"I wasn't even a year sober and a former school pal, Elvin Asher, came down and asked if I'd play in a bar band. I said, 'I don't play in taverns anymore.' A number of other people wanted me to come out and party, and I said, 'No, I don't do that anymore.'

"I played in four or five tavern bands [before his conversion to Christianity] but none of them lasted. Someone would get drunk and get into a fight," George said.

It soon was obvious to those who knew the old George LeMaster Jr. that this third detoxification effort was proving itself to be different from the other two. George LeMaster Jr., thanks to Jesus Christ, was a new man.

But his story doesn't end here. In fact, it only marked the place where a life reset took place. It was a new beginning.

Chapter 6

Another Avenue for Music

Friend and pastor Harry Miller talked to Melvin Gordy, a member of the Harold Shelton Gospel Group, and got George into the northeast Missouri gospel band.

"From the time I got out of the hospital, I couldn't do anything. People shepherded me. The Lord opened doors, and it was up to me to go through them," George said.

George ended up playing in the coed gospel group after meeting band leader Harold, an alcoholic turned pastor. George was band member number 13, playing backup rhythm guitar.

"Before Harold had organized the gospel band, he had been a drinker and ran moonshine. I told him, 'You don't want me in your band. I just came off alcoholism.' Harold insisted I play along with 'I Saw the Light.'"

Perhaps there was no more fitting song explaining George's conversion.

"He asked the band what they thought of me, and I was accepted. We played on the road five days a week."

George was in the Harold Shelton band from 1982 to 1987.

"I noticed that when you played for the Lord, you were more at ease. At a bar, the first thing you would do, you'd size everything up. Harold had played [in the past] at dances, where alcohol and fights were common. He noted that playing for the Lord was better too.

"Harold had [previously] been a drinker, and God got ahold of him [apparently in the late 1940s]. He drove a coal truck, and his drinking interfered with his job enough that the boss gave him the ultimatum—to stop drinking or lose his job.

"We played at nursing homes, food centers, parks, and even a gun and dog show."

Gun and dog shows were common at rural Rutledge and Colony in Knox County, Missouri, where flea market items were also sold, as were various dogs. The flea markets continue one weekend a month from April to October.

One summer day, Shelton's band played in the Memphis Missouri town square, thirty-seven miles west of Wayland. A performer (or group) since forgotten asked for someone from Shelton's group to play guitar as their player was sick. George was chosen to play guitar for them.

George played a half-hour as the Shelton band waited for him. He was offered $45 for his effort. Since the Shelton band didn't charge, George didn't feel right taking pay and declined it.

Robert John and Ada LeMaster, George LeMaster Jr.'s paternal grandparents.

This was a Wayland, Missouri, gas station in 1953. From *left* are town barber Happy Kerns, Willard Cooey, (*seated, partially hidden*), George Willis LeMaster Sr., Tom Ferguson (*hidden*), and young George William LeMaster Jr.

Family members show a good fish catch this day in June 1974. From *left* are an ill George LeMaster Jr.; George LeMaster Sr.; and a brother-in-law to George Jr., Chester South.

George LeMaster Jr.'s uncle Walter Lee LeMaster, aka Sagebrush Sandy, at *left*; guitarist and eventual George LeMaster Jr. bar-playing pal Don Johnson at *right*; and an unidentified KOKX radio personality with a desk full of fan mail.

Sagebrush Sandy and his horse Flash in a 1960s promotional photo.

George LeMaster Jr. was a security guard in 1979 at a movie theater before being reassigned to Shelor Globe in Keokuk, Iowa.

George LeMaster Jr. (*left*) saved and now alcohol-free, is pictured with spiritual mentor, pastor, and gospel band leader Harold Shelton in 1982.

The Harold Shelton Gospel Group band in 1987. Band members from *left: row 1* are Rodney Brown, Bill Bloom, and George LeMaster Jr.; *row 2* are Irene Butler, Frances Shelton, and Neva Adamson; and *row 3* are Elmer Privia, Bob Adams, Henrietta Privia, band namesake Harold Shelton, Cora Brown, Melvin Gordy, and Joyce McColm.

George LeMaster Jr. holds his ordination certificate with ceremony participants Rev. Barney Lollar (*left*) and Rev. Earl V. Elliot (*right*).

George and Linda LeMaster hold his ordination certificate January 30, 1989, with artistic representations of their mutual best friend, Jesus Christ, on the wall.

Family members of George LeMaster Jr. at his ordination to the gospel ministry included his parents and two siblings. From *left* are George LeMaster Sr., sister Connie Handyside, his mother Mary LeMaster, George Jr.; sister Carla South, and husband Chester South.

Another family picture at George Jr.'s 1989 ordination includes George Jr., his wife, their children, and his parents. From *left* are his mother Mary LeMaster, son Robert LeMaster, George Jr., Robert Wood and his wife (George and Linda's daughter) Mary LeMaster Wood, son George V. LeMaster III, and George LeMaster Sr.

At the church ordination and pictured in the kitchen are church members Neva Adamson; her granddaughter Ty Anne Ray; George and Linda LeMaster; and Pat Shelton, daughter of the late pastor Harold Shelton.

Left: This is the exterior of the Luray, Missouri Full Gospel Church circa the late 1990s. The building has since been abandoned due to falling into need of repair.

Right: George Jr. and Linda LeMaster are pictured outside the door of the Luray, Missouri, Full Gospel Church in 1998.

The St. Francisville Missouri Toll Bridge into Iowa ceased as such on December 6, 2004. Those employed at its closing were (from *left*) Tom Logsdon, Larry Broomhall Sr., George LeMaster Sr., Millie Phillips, Eleanora Hudson, Winston Walker, Jim Elder, Lori Nevies, Lewis Edlen, Chester South, and George LeMaster Jr.

The Chambersburg Church Bell now rests in a shed near the Chambersburg, Missouri, Protestant cemetery. This is near where the church once stood.

Left: George and Linda LeMaster, August 2007. *Right:* George and Linda LeMaster, May 2021.

Chapter 7

Transition Years

From 1982 to 1990, there were a lot of changes going on in George LeMaster Jr.'s life. He had odd jobs at this time and played with Shelton's band.

The Harold Shelton Gospel Group band was on the road five days a week.

Generally, they went out on Mondays and were back for Tuesday night Bible studies. Then, Wednesdays through Fridays, the group would perform and be back for Saturday night church and then Sunday services. Then a similar schedule was usually repeated.

Harold Shelton lived in Luray, Missouri but pastored the churches of Carmel [seven miles south of 136 on Route BB in Clark County] and Chambersburg [on Route NN] in Clark County as well.

Carmel Church had a partition. The women sat on one side, men on the other.

Chambersburg Church had been of Methodist denomination affiliation but became a nondenominational church when Harold Shelton was pastor.

Luray Full Gospel Church was formed in 1960 when Shelton began preaching. It was located in the former MWA building [standing for Modern Woodmen of America]. The building had other uses before Shelton turned it into a church.

Shelton took off the second story by adding a roof inside the structure first then removing the old roof and second story.

They intentionally planned to have the services on Saturday nights and Bible studies [then] on Tuesday so as not to interfere with the other Luray church meeting times of the more common Sunday and Wednesday nights.

Linda and George went with Shelton to his church in 1982. In those days, Luray was still somewhat of a bustling place, and Shelton had such a draw that some came from Carthage, Illinois, more than forty miles east. Some of the distant churchgoers may have been followers of Shelton's group.

There were big crowds in Luray on Saturday night that would go to the Heintz Cafe. George and Linda had trouble finding a place to park near the church. Occasionally, some of the dinner crowd came to church afterward.

George LeMaster Jr. was indeed a changed man. Where he once despised being in church, he now was regularly attending it with Linda. Little did he know that God had other plans to make church important for him.

Chapter 8

A Taste of Preaching

"I backed into the ministry."

In traveling to the various venues, Harold would lead George with thoughts like:

HAROLD: Isn't that a beautiful sight?
GEORGE: It sure is.
HAROLD: Heaven is more beautiful...

"Then he would quote scripture, and I'd ask, 'Well, where is that?' and he'd say, 'In the book of Proverbs or wherever it was,' but he wouldn't tell me where other than the book of the Bible. He told me to read it and find it. Here is another man who molded me. This is when things started popping out of the Bible at me when I needed it. At that time, I didn't know it was the Holy Spirit working."

In 1982, when George joined Harold Shelton's gospel group, he and Linda went to Shelton's church. A year or two after George began playing with Shelton's band, he was baptized into the faith in a farm pond on Shelton's farm.

"I had had religious experiences. I was sprinkled as a child, but I didn't go under [baptism by immersion in 1982] until I hung around with Harold. I had [previously] had enough with religion to make me uncomfortable. I was a late bloomer. I didn't come to Jesus until after the dump [experience].

"It was a feeling of completeness," George Jr. said.

That's not to say George's life was perfect. Once, George was doing mechanical work under Harold's truck with fellow band member Bill Bloom, who hit the muffler with a hammer.

"Rust fell off in my face. I swore and looked up and there was Harold. After a few awkward seconds, he said, 'Did that help?'

"I said, 'No, but the rust hurt my eyes.' That's all Harold ever said about that incident.

"Once, Harold had to go to a wedding or funeral, and he asked me to take over the pulpit. I said, 'I'm no preacher.' Harold said, 'Just tell them what God is doing.'"

In 1987, perhaps in August, former alcoholic George LeMaster Jr. preached on John 14:6, "Jesus is the way, the only way."

When George was still an alcoholic, he probably would not have felt that way about Jesus. But God is able to change people.

"I'd say I was nervous before, but when I got in the pulpit, God took over. Doors were opening now," George said.

"Twice I filled in for him, and then I offered to fill in anytime he was gone," George continued.

Occasionally, there were band jam sessions apart from scheduled concert and church activities of the Shelton Gospel Group. Many jam sessions were in Luray and enjoyed by church members and community members alike.

One such jam session, on Friday, June 26, 1987, during a community event at Luray, the Harold Shelton Gospel Group was playing and singing in a carport near the church. Things for the band changed that day in an instant.

"Harold came into the house, went in the bathroom, and fell. He had an aneurysm [burst]," Linda said.

"Perhaps he had premonitions. Harold used to say, 'Stay on the straight and narrow path. My race is almost done. I'm in the autumn of my life.' The year before he died, he told us of things that were important. He'd say, 'One hundred years from now, they will not know who you and I are now. Do things now, all for the Lord Jesus.'

"He had had the aneurysm in his abdomen for a while, but when it burst, he bled inside and swelled up like a poisoned pup," George said.

Shelton, age seventy-seven, died later that day in Keokuk Area Hospital.

"A lot of people gathered at the Keokuk Hospital lawn. One gal from the hospital came out and wondered who was in here, thinking it was a movie star, with the crowd," George said.

For two and a half years, George also tried to keep Harold's band going. Their bylaws said they would play without charge, but when he found out some band members had charged to play, George quickly severed his ties to the band.

Bill Bloom, George, and maybe another band member occasionally played for the churches Shelton pastored.

He had learned of the charging when someone asked how he wanted his share of the money.

"We were playing and singing for the Lord's glory, not for our praise or money," George said.

He said others in the gospel group were convinced they could make it in Nashville, to which George scoffed.

"They [Nashville music climate] would eat us alive," he said, sensing a cutthroat music business that was not for the faint of heart.

When George left, the band broke up.

Chapter 9

Shelton's Churches

With the death of Harold Shelton, the questions of pastoring his churches, and maybe even the future of the three churches themselves, were in limbo.

"I got to leaning on the man. He was my idol. I put too much emphasis on Harold and not enough on Jesus Christ. When he suddenly passed in 1987, I was lost. I offered to fill in as pastor until they got someone to do that."

Two other prospective candidates came to apply for the preacher's job. Neither was approved by the church. Nor did Harold's three churches search actively for anyone other than George LeMaster Jr. to replace Harold.

Filling in was okay, but it wasn't on George's radar to become a regular pastor. George expected it to be a short-term service until a regular preacher came along. It has lasted much longer than he thought it would.

Neva Adamson and her husband James helped build the Luray Full Gospel Church. When James died, Neva stepped into James' church board positions and became a strong proponent of ordaining George.

By October 1987, George expressed his desire to be ordained into the ministry. In a letter from Pat Shelton's mother Frances to Pat, she said if George was ready, to contact a Luther Davis, who would set up the ordination. Davis, a member of Victory Fellowship Church in Iowa, was a close friend of Harold and Frances Shelton.

"Along in November 1988, I was asked if I wished to be ordained. We [church board members Delbert Boley, Neva Adamson, Melvin Gordy, and Dean Phillips] said they would bring it to a congregation vote. Brother Harold's wife, Frances, recommended my ordination, and after a meeting with Brother Barney Lollar and Brother Earl Elliot from the Victory Fellowship Church in Brighton, Iowa, it was agreed.

On January 30, 1989, George William LeMaster Jr. was ordained to the ministry of the Full Gospel Church.

Both George's mother and father were among those present at his ordination service, as were several siblings, his wife Linda, and their three children.

"Mom always said I was going to be a preacher. She lived long enough to see it happen. At the ordination, she said, 'I told you so.'"

May Beth LeMaster died three days short of the fifth anniversary of George's ordination.

"I told them [the Luray congregation] 'I'm not perfect. I'm a shepherd. Don't put me on a pedestal. I can fall, and when preachers fall, they fall hard."

George still remembered the sour taste he had from some preachers of the past and some congregational expectations of the ministers.

One time, after George became the pastor, he was doing outside work on the church. George went to the nearby Heintz Café to take a break. The waitress offered him water or Coke to refresh himself. Church member James Adamson was already seated with a coffee.

One man named Glen (not real name) came in and complained of the Luray Full Gospel Church being the *drunkard's church* because Harold Shelton and now George LeMaster Jr. had been drunks before Jesus changed them.

The waitress egged on the critic. George sat silently, sipping his Coke.

"I hear the pastor [George] is really nice," the waitress said.

Yet the man continued to criticize the church.

"I hadn't been saved that long and still could have been a problem. I thanked her for the drink and went outside. She continued talking to the man."

George, with his ire rising, knew to leave before he became a problem. Had he stayed, he feared his actions would have reflected badly on his Savior, to say nothing of how it would turn out for Glen.

"The waitress came over to the church later and said, 'You should have stayed. It got better.' I knew I needed to avoid the confrontation. She said, 'After you left, I asked if he knew the preacher of the Luray Full Gospel Church, and he said, 'No.' She said, 'He was the man sitting by you who left.' Glen shut up.

"I was only trying to keep the church going for a place to come into on Saturday nights. You could come wearing your everyday clothes."

George once went to the Luray post office after Harold's death to get the address changed from Harold's to his.

"The people in Luray come here and see that I was different than what they heard of me [of the changes through Christ].

"One time in a Luray church service, as we were finishing, a drunk man came from the tavern waving a $100 bill that he won on a bet whether he would step into the church. I asked him, 'Whom does that belong to?' He said, 'What do you mean?' I said, 'What are you going to do with it? I'll tell the tavern you were here, but what are you going to do with that?' He never answered what he would do with it."

George's point was that even a drunkard can come to Christ, and it's no big deal if the guy won a bet and entered a church building.

George and Linda later said that man with the $100 bill was close to making a decision for Christ after this incident but neither knows for sure if that happened.

"I look at ministry as a team effort. If I miss someone, maybe someone else will say the right thing at the right time with the right attitude.

"I tried to keep his [Harold's] three churches—Carmel, Chambersburg, and Luray—going. Luray was the mother church."

Carmel Church and Chambersburg Church had reopened at the request of elderly former members after being closed for a time. Carmel closed in 1989 with four people. The building, which was in a pasture anyway, was razed and is an expanded farm field.

"At Chambersburg, it took about all the money of the church to fill the propane tank. I went to turn on the furnace once, and it shut off. I thought it was a thermocouple issue. We found that someone had been siphoning propane from the church's tank. We asked the cemetery board to borrow $75 to fill the tank until our next offering. They said, 'If you can't keep it up, close the church.'"

The Chambersburg Church, which near the end had fifteen in attendance, closed shortly after that in 1991, and the building was sold and moved, becoming a private house some fifteen miles away. Reportedly—and oddly a surprise when George found out— George's picture is still on the wall of the church-turned-residence as he was the pastor when the church closed.

The church bell was left near the cemetery as the only remembrance of a church presence in Chambersburg, an unincorporated area in extreme northern Clark County, Missouri.

"I took it to mean that they cared more for the dead than the living," Linda said.

George learned that when Chambersburg was platted, there were two cemeteries because Catholics and Protestants then couldn't get along. The bell is near the Protestant cemetery. The lot where the church once set is a vacant lot between the bell and the cemetery toolshed.

But with the closing of the two churches, George found doors opening.

"I had trouble finding a job before and even after because I had been a drunk."

George worked at River City Metals from 1981 to 1985; he played in Shelton's band and did odd jobs for several years.

After Thomas Truck closed, Donnie Gillpin was also a fellow employee at River City Metals where ten-, twelve-, and fourteen-foot diameter satellite dishes were made. Donnie, who had tried to witness to George, now joined George in trying to witness to other River City Metal coworkers.

George got a job in 2001 as a toll taker for the St. Francisville Missouri Bridge, which allowed traffic to and from Iowa over the Des Moines River. George was employed there until it closed in 2004, three and a half years later.

"Eleanora Hudson, treasurer for the Wayland Special Road District which operated the toll bridge, said, 'You are sober enough this time. We think we can trust you.' I said, 'Can you trust me with the money?' She said, 'We could have trusted you when you were drinking. We knew you were not a thief.'"

The road district is also the same group that built a concrete, low-river crossing in the 1960s, which was ironically located on the way to the city dump. The concrete crossing prevented washouts and kept farm equipment like combines from getting stuck in the dirt.

George LeMaster Sr. was also employed as a toll taker at the bridge, and occasionally, father and son worked a shift together.

"It was interesting working with Dad. We were a lot alike, so we kind of thought alike on many things."

Other than the Morris Garage of years past, the father and son LeMasters didn't work together for any other employer.

The St. Francisville Toll Bridge, built in 1937, was 763 feet long and 21.7 feet wide with three main spans and six approach spans. It was a rare cantilever truss bridge following a Warren truss configuration. In the early 2000s, the bridge was bypassed with Missouri State Route 27 (SR-27) and became part of the Avenue of the Saints, connecting St. Louis, Missouri with St. Paul, Minnesota.

Because of the new bridge carrying four-lane traffic to and from Iowa, the toll bridge became a free bridge in 2003, and in 2016 was closed to all traffic, perhaps due to extensive cracking of piers. Until it became a free bridge, it was operated by the Wayland Special Road District.[3]

George Jr. also drove for Auto Zone parts from 2004 to 2011 after the toll bridge closed.

---

[3] Some of the bridge information came from the website Historicbridge.org.

One friend of George's saw him after he sobered up and was surprised, thinking George Jr. had already died from alcoholism.

"I told him, 'I was dead, but now I'm alive in Christ. I had a chance to witness to him before he went to be home with the Lord.

"You see the Lord working through the whole thing," George said.

Chapter 10

Family Reconciliation

While things were better in George's life with alcohol no longer a factor, he felt there was still some unfinished business with his family from the previous damage of the past alcoholism.

"Linda stuck with me through the hell. Linda kept the kids in the church. I had been at home either getting sober or getting drunk again."

After George started preaching in 1987, he had a *come-to-Jesus meeting* with his wife and children around the kitchen table to clear the air.

"I told the kids to tell me what they have felt [about me]. I wasn't asking for their forgiveness. I just wanted them to get it out of their system."

The result was honestly agonizing yet therapeutic. Here is a summary of their responses.

"Mary, the oldest, told me she wasn't able to bring her friends home because I was always drunk. George III said he didn't like me. Robert is like me and holds things in.

"What they said was painful to hear but long overdue, and I deserved it. I was in the pulpit saying Jesus Christ is the way, but I had dirty laundry I needed to get rid of.

"I'll own up to what I've been, a drunk, but I did not gamble, and I did not cheat on my wife. Most of the women in the bar don't get better looking [after drinking, despite songs to the contrary]. I saw too many fights in the tavern. Also, what self-respecting woman wants a drunk man?"

It's an ironic question knowing Linda for years had a drunk man.

As for the time before George got saved, Linda gave him the choice: "The bottle or me?" George had chosen *the bottle*; why didn't Linda leave him then after his answer?

"Because I loved him. But I didn't like him," she said after pausing through tears to collect her thoughts. "He didn't beat me, except maybe with words when he was inebriated, but I knew that wasn't really him. I figured if I left, it would be the end of him."

"It would have been," George agreed softly.

The children, through the years, have become more accepting of George.

"Time heals the wounds," George said.

"Mom asked if I could see the change in Dad [when he stopped drinking], and I said, 'Yes.' Right after he quit, he and Mom would study the Bible together. He read it more after Mom died."

"The whole family had been after me to quit [after my father did]."

May Beth LeMaster likely saw the change in her husband and wanted it for her son as well.

When the junior eventually gave up drinking, too, he told his dad something to the effect of finding a Bible in the city dump. He didn't mention the suicide plans then.

"I didn't want people to know I was a failure. My family had previously felt suicide was the unpardonable sin because there was no opportunity to repent from it."

His parents likely found out about the suicide plan at the dump that God foiled when George started speaking about the little red book. He doesn't recall their reaction.

"Dad had been talking with Lester and said Lester was a good influence on me. Him and Harry Miller.

"I told Dad I found Jesus. He said, 'Are you sure this time?'"

George Jr. was sure.

While George wanted to share Jesus with known sinners, he didn't immediately share it with family.

"I figured my family already knew about Jesus. I wanted to tell the drunks who didn't know. I had the misconception that when people go to church, they are already saved."

He said because of Christ, his relationship with his siblings has drawn them closer.

After George Jr. was ordained to the gospel ministry, his father would ask *him* where various verses were. Maybe he was testing George Jr.'s knowledge, or maybe he thought the ordination suddenly made his son a Bible scholar. That's not necessarily the case in ordination, and for George, there was no formal Bible college training.

"He thought I was smart. I was just using my concordance," George Jr. said.

George said he was also fond of his mother-in-law, Helen South, who never spoke ill of him, even at his worst.

"She never gave up on me or nagged me. I found out later she helped Linda and the kids with money quite a few times. She truly was a wonderful mother-in-law. I don't do mother-in-law jokes because mine was good."

Chapter 11

Telling the Story

It was eight years after George LeMaster Jr. found the New Testament in the dump when George was telling the story of the purpose of the Bible that Linda first learned of the planned suicide that Valentine's Day in 1982.

"In May 1990, while our gospel group was performing, I had the privilege of meeting and hearing Gideon representative Donald Waterman speak at Bear Creek Baptist Church—now defunct—near Wyaconda, Missouri.

"They were having a church homecoming for all the former residents. We [Harold Shelton's gospel group] were playing. I didn't go to the homecoming to talk. Don Waterman was at that meeting. He was explaining the different-colored New Testament covers.

"It was warm out, and I mentioned it to Don at that meeting. I looked at his red Bible. I related my experience to him of how the *little red book* had influenced my life.

"He said, 'That's very interesting. You need to tell others about that.' I think that's about the time Neva Adamson [of the Luray Full Gospel Church] found out about my story."

Donald Waterman was a member of the Clark and Lewis County, Missouri Camp of the Gideons International, which distributed New Testaments like the red Bible George found and thousands more New Testaments of various colored covers and full Bibles through the organization.

The Gideons International, based in Nashville, Tennessee, has member volunteers of various denominations passing out New Testaments with various colored covers, each color reflecting the intended audience [medical, children, military, etc.].

Generally, orange-covered New Testaments are given in sidewalk distributions. Green is for college and university students. Red is for in-school middle and high school students. Camouflage is for the military. Dark blue is for the non-English language. White is for medical professionals. Light blue is distributed by Gideon auxiliary members. Brown is for personal distribution. Burgundy is for personal Gideon testaments for witnessing. Periwinkle is for the personal witnessing of auxiliary members.

They also place full Bibles in prisons, hotels, and other places.

George's story sparked Waterman's interest because of the obvious tie to the Gideons.

"I was ashamed of what I planned to do and did not want to reflect badly on Linda and the family. Before Christ got ahold of me, I was a very private person. I still am to a certain degree. I'm not proud of the dump experience," he said.

But Don was interested in George's story for it was a testimony to the power of God's Word to change the worst of conditions and offer new hope.

Before he passed away in 2004, Waterman also pastored, at various times, in Southern Baptist Fellowship Church in Wayland, Alexandria (Missouri) Baptist, and Greentop (Missouri) Baptist.

The Gideons have lots of stories of people changed by God's Word, but George LeMaster Jr.'s story is arguably among one of the more powerful and unique.

"It wasn't long after that, that someone Don Waterman knew in Racine, Wisconsin asked me to come and tell my story. It was interesting how God was working. At Racine, I was as nervous as all get out. I flew from Quincy, Illinois to Racine. I was met by a Gideon handler at the airport, taken to the hotel, and then to the meeting.

"My handler said, 'Don't be nervous. Just give your testimony.'

"I had heard that in Wisconsin, people were clannish, but when I left, I felt I was accepted. They treated me like royalty."

Fifty to sixty people heard George LeMaster Jr. at a Wisconsin-Upper Michigan State Convention meeting in April 1991.

"This was the first time I gave the testimony [out of Clark County], and the first time I ever flew," George said.

This began years of occasional traveling, mainly to hundreds of Gideons' meetings, to tell how their corporate work saved one simple man from Wayland, Missouri who planned to leave the city dump not of his own accord.

Most of the sixty or so talks he has given have been at Gideon pastor-appreciation events, but some of them were at churches where George was invited to speak, and sometimes the day after a Saturday Gideons' meeting.

"After the Wisconsin speech, I gave the Bible to Don to use in his travels and distributions for the Gideons. I know he later took it to Belarus. Don Waterman had done some missionary work in the early 1990s."

Southern Baptists had a partnership with Belarus at that time, and Waterman went there as a dairy cattle farmer; he had several decades of experience with the animals but used the agriculture opportunities to witness about his Lord and Savior.

He carried the red Bible that brought George out of the dump alive and pointed him to Jesus Christ with him to Belarus.

Don told of George's story, and a lady in Belarus asked to see the Bible.

At that time, Belarus was restricted to Bible distribution. Don thought he had given too much information and was being set up by undercover agents out to squelch the gospel and go after the messenger.

Waterman talked to a pastor or a facilitator in Belarus, who said the woman was not part of the KGB or the Belarus equivalent to such a group. He confirmed she was just curious about the Word of God. Don then went to the motel and got the pocket New Testament out of his luggage.

"Don had a feel for the people. He showed the red Bible to the woman, and tears started streaming down her cheeks. They didn't have a lot of Bibles over there," George said.

"Don told her, 'This is the Word of God that saved that man's life [George]. It saves other people's lives. That's what the Word of God does.'"

Don said several other people came around and talked about that Bible.

"They were hungry for the Word of God and can't get it. We have multiple Bibles [in the United States of America], and people don't want it," George said.

"Don said he used the red Bible when he traveled on distributions and used my testimony. Don said then that the day he died, the Bible would pass through the ranks of Gideons.

"I said, 'That's fine.' I didn't keep the Bible because it did what it was supposed to do, and now it still goes out," George said.

Don Waterman set up other local meetings in Kahoka and Memphis and other Missouri places. George also spoke in Iowa, Louisiana, and Arkansas. Meetings in Des Moines, Iowa, and one since forgotten Missouri location were state Gideon gatherings.

The Gideon meetings George traveled to, accompanied by Linda when she could, have been uplifting. Linda hadn't been able to attend all he did because of her job and other commitments.

However, at one Missouri event, the facility only had food for about twenty-five people and some seventy-five attended. George said his pork chops "couldn't be cut with a chain saw."

Linda reminded him, "But the people of the Gideons were nice, and they had met a lot of good people."

"The Gideons never made me feel less than I was. We found people are the same all over," Linda said.

At another Missouri meeting in a prestigious large city hotel, George and Linda were looked down on by the hotel staff, who would not wait on them immediately, apparently because he was in his travel clothes—T-shirt and blue jeans.

George was on the verge of returning to Wayland and at the last minute called the person who invited him to speak. That man called the hotel and got the attention of management. The hotel staff then came and *gushed* all over George and Linda.

Again, they found nothing but kindness among the Gideons' representatives.

"They were Christian," Linda said of Gideons' representatives.

It should be expected that a Christian organization like the Gideons would act like Christians.

At one speaking engagement in November 1994 in Ankeny, Iowa, George was using a restroom after the meal and before sharing his testimony when the man at the next urinal—of all places—began a conversation.

"He asked if I knew Jesus. I told him, 'Yes.' He said, 'I just wanted to know if you knew. I'm a saved Jew. I like to talk to my Jewish brethren.' I said, 'I'm Protestant.' We both laughed."

The man saying he was *a saved Jew* confused George at the time.

"Mom was instrumental in godly training in the home. She said, 'You don't want to say anything against the Jews. They are God's chosen people.'"

George had assumed that because they were *God's chosen people*, all Jews were saved. He has since come to learn that neither profession of a denomination nor church attendance nor church membership nor even being *one of God's chosen people* automatically made one a believer.

After the visit with the messianic Jew, George saw him in the audience as he spoke. Afterward, he came up and asked for my address and said he'd send cookies.

"He did send them," George recalled, his eyes lighting up at the memory.

Living a somewhat sheltered life in Wayland meant learning new things about the world in his travels, such as Jews—like Gentiles—needing to be saved. But that was not all George has learned in his travels.

"I had done a speech in Lake Charles, Louisiana in November 1991 for the Louisiana State Gideons Convention. It was just after Halloween, and the temperature got to forty-six degrees early in the morning. I went to the lobby, and there were two women there in parkas. I had a few minutes to wait for my handler in that city, so I walked a couple of blocks to look at flowers still in bloom.

73

"A lady came running after me. She was concerned because I went to another parish. I was thinking denomination, and she was thinking county. The Louisiana handler arrived and confirmed the woman's concern.

"[To them] you are a [censored word] Yankee. They'd run you in for anything, even spitting on the sidewalk, just because you are from out of town. I guar-ron-tee it," his Cajun handler said.

When he had picked up George at the airport in Louisiana, the handler had said he could be identified by *a flowery hat*.

"His flowery hat did stand out. I was told not to say anything about Marie Laveau. She was a voodoo priestess who has been dead for a hundred years, and she is still worshipped. He [my Cajun handler] also said to stay away from the graveyard and the hey-you-call-its. He later explained he was talking about ghosts, spirits."

In a passing conversation, George asked about Mardi Gras. His Cajun handler said, "Don't go, but if you do, stay only on Bourbon Street. You go down another street, they'll slit your throat and take everything from you. It's debauchery at Mardi Gras that will make even a sinner blush."

In October 1996, George spoke at an Arkansas event and was invited to speak at a small rural area at the Martin Chapel Assembly of God Church, also in Arkansas, the next day. George agreed as long as he could meet his flight home on time.

The handler at this Arkansas event met George that Sunday morning in a Ford Ranger truck to take the hills.

"I call them mountains. That Ford never got out of second gear. He got to a church in the hills and told me to wait in the pickup truck, and he'd be back. There was no one around the church. After a few minutes, the man came back with the preacher. I got out of the truck, and we started talking.

"You are from the north, aren't you?" the preacher asked George.

"Yes, I am," George replied.

"You giving your testimony?" the preacher asked.

"Yes, I am," George said.

This Arkansas handler walked a little with George as the preacher left, and suddenly, there were fifteen to twenty people on the street.

"They came from nowhere. The preacher wanted me to meet with the elders. I did and then sat in the adult Sunday school class. Then that little church filled up completely with people."

"We've got a problem. I don't know how to take you," the preacher said.

George was confused.

"You're not a fed [federal agent] are you?"

"No," George said, surprised by the question.

"The boys on the mountain make this stuff," the preacher said.

George understood he was talking about moonshine.

"Alcohol is a problem all over," George said.

The preacher said he would not be near the pulpit when George spoke. He wanted to see the response of some of the congregation.

The preacher's action may have also been in anticipating a need for crowd control. It was not needed. George spoke and was later welcomed to come back to the church and congregation anytime.

"My handler said I did well. I said I was only saying what God told me to say. The handler said, 'Some of the guys don't have their liver. They've been drinking [moonshine] since they were young.' I asked him why he didn't tell me all this sooner. He said, 'I wasn't sure you'd agree to come up here.'"

Certainly, liverless moonshiners need to know Jesus, too, and it may not have mattered to George if he had found out beforehand.

George LeMaster Jr., decades later, still speaks when Gideons and other people want to hear his story.

At times, people come up to him after his talk to confide in their own or spouse's alcohol problem.

"There is a stigma concerning alcohol and drugs now," he said.

At one Gideon meeting in Keokuk, Iowa, George found himself in a locale where there used to be gambling and alcohol. Now he was telling people about Jesus. He pondered the irony and the wonder of the change the Holy Spirit can make.

Gideon meetings have comprised the bulk of George LeMaster Jr.'s talks about his testimony. Usually, they were about ten minutes long, and maybe he had a few minutes to briefly chat with others after the meetings. Often, there was no long testimony or visit time before or after a speech.

From 1991 to 2013, George spoke to at least sixty Midwestern events to share his story; many of them were pastor-appreciation meals sponsored by the Gideons. However, George is still willing to share his testimony with others who need to hear it if it will help one person turn to Christ.

One audience in the fall of 1991 was his Chambersburg congregation for a homecoming service they held.

He spoke in May of 1991 for a sixth-grade children's promotion at a Kahoka school. He was later asked if the words were appropriate for children. The gist of George's response was something like, "They ought to learn of the dangers now, and maybe it will keep them from making a similar mistake in their lives."

On August 19, 1995, he spoke at a Gideon event in West Memphis, Arkansas, and then was asked to speak the next morning at the West Memphis, Arkansas First Baptist Church. His talk helped the church raise over $2,000 for Gideon Bibles.

In his collection of the Gideon programs through the years are also some cards sent by Gideon members. People can send Gideon Bibles in honor or in memory of a party. In the cards George received, individuals who heard his talk purchased one to five Bibles for the Gideons. These purchased Bibles are given by the Gideons.

Because of his talks, several dozen Bibles have gone out in honor of George's testimony. God only knows whose lives were reached by the Bibles, which went out because George shared his testimony.

In June 2011, he spoke at Jerseyville, Illinois where their local camp was holding its first pastor's appreciation event.

His speeches have been given—so far and in no particular order—in the Missouri communities of Kahoka, Chambersburg, Hannibal, Shelbina, Canton, Moberly, Gray Summit, Bowling Green, Festus, Memphis, Fulton, Fayette, St. Peters, Kirksville, Jefferson City, Chillicothe, St. Joseph, and Wentzville.

In Illinois, he has spoken in Macomb, Carthage, Collinsville, Nauvoo, Chester, and Jerseyville. In Iowa, he has shared the testimony in Ankeny, Des Moines, Waterloo, Burlington, Keokuk, Mt. Pleasant, and Iowa City.

Racine is the lone Wisconsin testimony speech site. Likewise, Lake Charles is the only one in Louisiana where the testimony has been shared. In Arkansas, he has been to West Memphis and Jonesboro.

At some of the Kahoka pastor-appreciation events, George and Linda have been there as pastor and wife, but even at one of those, another speaker borrowed George's testimony, with his permission.

Talks in Iowa, Wisconsin, Louisiana, Illinois, and Missouri included state Gideon conventions.

Chapter 12

Another Deliverance

Although miraculously delivered from alcoholism, George LeMaster Jr. had another longtime vice with which he was dealing—smoking.

On January 14, 1993, George had finished a Gideon talk at the Mark Twain Hotel in downtown Hannibal, Missouri. He was outside smoking a cigarette.

"Hey. Are you the speaker?" the unknown Gideon asked him.

George admitted he was. He said he never tried to hide his smoking.

On the way home, he was driving; Linda was sleeping, preparing for an early wake-up call to go to work. George lit another cigarette, and this one was different from any other he had smoked.

"It felt like fire down in the lungs. I'd never had that before. I rolled down the window and threw out the cigarette. Then I reached in the pocket and found the rest of the pack and threw them out the window too. The next few days were rough."

Why George suddenly decided to quit smoking, no one may ever know. Perhaps it was the unknown Gideon, bothered by seeing a smoker, the same one who had given a fine testimony of alcohol deliverance, who may have been praying for George. Maybe Linda was praying. Maybe it was both. Maybe there was another unknown factor.

A week later, on January 21, 1993, George delivered another Gideon pastor's appreciation speech at the Skyway Café in Shelbina, Missouri. Linda had accompanied him.

"I asked Linda how my testimony went [at Shelbina]. She said it was *okay*. I said, 'If anyone had touched me, I would have ripped their head off.' I was so wound up and the draw of nicotine was so strong."

Linda posed an important question to her husband, "Did you ask the Lord to help you?"

The question left George stunned about the obvious answer. God had helped him with so much and brought deliverance from the decades-long alcoholism. He knew how in prayer to ask God. But the truth is, he had *not* asked God for help in stopping smoking.

After they got home, they prayed together for a few days.

"He could have delivered me earlier. I just never asked. Linda is my rock that I lean on," George said.

George LeMaster Jr.'s last cigarette was that January 14, 1993, on the way home from Hannibal, where inhaling left a painful message.

Chapter 13

Paying It Forward

In October 1996 at another Saturday night, this time in the auditorium of Arkansas State University, West Memphis, Arkansas, George spoke before some three hundred people at a Gideons pastor's appreciation event.

"I think it was the first time speaking in an auditorium that used the ceiling floodlights. I could only see the crowd so far because of the lights.

"In the hallway, after the speech, as people were leaving, a man came up to me. He said, 'I heard your testimony. Your testimony is my life.'"

The man had permission to run the lights and sound in the auditorium but had trouble holding on to jobs because of his own alcohol addiction.

George said the man told the effects of his own drinking problem—he was about to lose his job; his wife was ready to divorce him and leave him and would have taken the kids with her.

It surely sounded like a story of which George was all too familiar—that of his own past life.

"I said, 'Jesus can help you. You need to turn your life over to him.' He said, 'I like to drink.' I told him, 'I had liked it, too, but I got to the place I could not handle it anymore.' He said, 'I can't lay it down.' I said, 'Let's have a word of prayer for the Lord to deliver you.' I prayed for peace, his family, and I think I said something like, 'Give this man what you gave me. Amen.'

"He was hurting the way I had hurt [before his own conversion]."

This prayer of deliverance was similar to what Lester Piersee helped George pray in his den fourteen years earlier.

However, a campus security guard saw the two men praying in the hallway and quickly approached them.

"Hey! You can't stand in the hallway and pray. You have to be in the auditorium because that's what they [Gideons] paid for. I said, 'We just did [pray]'. I wasn't trying to be smart about it. The guard said, 'You can't proselyte in the hallway.' I said, 'We're done here,' and I shook the hands of the man in the hallway.

"I asked the officer if he was going to detain me. He said, 'No, just move on.'"

The handler came and found George, who recounted the story of the security cop, and agreed the school didn't like unplanned prayer in the hallways, a thought common among secular institutions.

When George got out of the car, his handler in that city told his wife, and they all had a laugh at George saying, "We just did" when told he couldn't pray.

That's the way a Christian ought to handle a situation. God isn't bound to the same rules of where prayer may be limited as set by mankind. As an active follower of Jesus Christ, George didn't know *not* to pray for a known need at the moment the need was revealed.

Some six months after the West Memphis speaking engagement, George got a phone call at his home from someone in Arkansas. The man identified himself, but George didn't immediately recognize the name.

"I was the guy you prayed with in the hallway. I called to let you know I'm back with my family. I got a job to support my family. I'm back in church with my family. I quit drinking, but it was a struggle.

"He said, The Lord helped George, and he's going to help me."

The two shared a few more joyful minutes on the phone.

"His wife mirrored mine. She was the strong one like Linda was for me. The man admitted, 'This [alcohol-free life] was a whole lot better than before.'"

Chapter 14

Music Has Another Verse

As diabetes robbed Mary of her eyesight, George Sr. continued reading the Bible to her.

In January 1994, Mary, "May Beth" LeMaster went to be with the Lord.

Once while dating again, George Sr. tried to hide his age by coloring his hair.

A truck driver crossing the Des Moines River was baffled to learn of two George LeMasters working the St. Francisville Bridge Toll Booth. Occasionally, they worked the same shift.

"Your hair is gray with black streaks, and your father's is dark brown. But he is older…" the truck driver asked in confusion.

George Jr. said his father had dyed his hair, explaining the difference between the two family members. The younger LeMaster didn't try coloring his hair.

One time, the hair dying didn't go well. He used a product that was supposed to gradually remove the gray, only, as George Jr. noted, "It turned his hair as orange as a carrot."

George Sr. went to be with the Lord on August 5, 2013.

Music had long been a part of George Jr.'s life—music at home, playing bars, then after being saved, playing with Shelton's gospel group. There hadn't been much in the way of regular playing in the gap since the band ceased.

Golden Age Ministries was formed around 2014. It included Clark County residents Kevin Eagle doing some lead guitar and some singing; Rev. Gary Whitaker, who would offer a devotion; and Rev. George LeMaster Jr. who played rhythm guitar and sang.

Golden Age Ministries had started with Gary, the chaplain at Country Aire Retirement Estates near Lewistown, Missouri, and got Kevin, who attended the same Freedom in Christ Church in Kahoka. At one service at Country Aire, George was asked to play backup rhythm guitar, did, and became part of the ministry group.

They regularly played at six nursing homes in Missouri—Lewis County Nursing Home; Canton, Country Aire; Clark County Nursing Home; Kahoka and Keokuk Convalescence Center and facilities in Montrose and Donnellson, Iowa. They also played for revivals and various other places where people wanted to hear gospel music.

Although not a performer, Linda is an integral part of the group. She encourages the residents, prays for and with them, talks with them, and shares a hug with them.

"Those are my people," she said.

One favorite song of nursing home residents was "Oh Come, Angel Band."

"That was kind of hard to sing with a lump in the throat," George said, thinking of Harold Shelton.

Before the 2020 COVID-19 pandemic shut things down, Jim Daw, a lead guitarist, was also with the group.

The Golden Age Ministry team previously went out among the nursing home crowds and took time to talk with the residents in more than just quick handshake greetings. One reason is that the band personally knew many of the senior citizens for whom they performed and knew them long before nursing home care was needed.

"The Lord had to be in it. Everything was working. It bothered the band when COVID-19 hit. Nursing homes were shut down."

The pandemic was not only difficult for the Golden Age Ministries band members but also for residents so used to seeing the attentive band themselves as nursing homes were closed to outsiders.

George and the other two of the band loved playing at several northeast Missouri nursing homes and came to know many more of the residents as friends, and often some were already friends.

"We did five or six nursing homes a month."

"They got to know us, and we got to know them. We were like an extended family. When you lose one of them, it hurts. Some people passed, and we weren't able to go to the funerals because of COVID-19 restrictions," George said.

On April 29, 2021, Kevin, Jim, and George had a jam session to reconnect and share music again. Several other Clark County-area musicians showed up. Gary was in ill health at the time, but they were hopeful Golden Age Ministries would again be able to play for senior citizens as nursing homes opened when COVID-19 restrictions were eased. Gary died on August 27, 2021.

George kept in practice by playing hymns on some Sunday evenings at the Southern Baptist Fellowship Church in Wayland, just two blocks from the LeMaster home.

However, even though COVID-19 restrictions were easing, by mid-2021 they were still waiting for nursing homes to further open up again to allow the residents to be blessed and the group to be able to bless those residing and working in the homes. There was concern with a resurgence of COVID-19 that nursing homes might close again, which again would be detrimental to the band and the nursing home residents.

Chapter 15

Life Now

George LeMaster Jr. has now been saved more years than he was a drunk.

"My life is a tapestry. You see the picture, but you can't see all the threads woven until you see the back," he said, indicating that life now has lots of threads from the past marvelously woven together.

In 2021, more than three decades after George LeMaster Jr. was named the *interim* Luray Full Gospel Church pastor, he was still preaching at the Luray Full Gospel Church, which shares facilities with the Luray Baptist Church. The Full Gospel congregation used the music room Saturday nights, and the Baptists used the sanctuary on Sundays.

In 2017, it was determined the structure of the Luray Full Gospel Church was unsafe due to its age—over a century old. The 12 × 12 floor beams were rotted so much that the piano jostled when one approached the piano. There also was no water or restroom.

"The Luray Baptist Church [also with a dwindling congregation] had a room that wasn't being used and offered to let us use their space for our services. Praise God," George said.

George said the issue was put to prayer a year before the two congregations agreed to share a building. Full Gospel pays a regular donation instead of rent.

Before the move, George had to get a raccoon that fled from the handles of an upright piano to a gas stove pipe. He forced it out, emptying several cans of air freshener into a pipe until the raccoon fell out.

"He [the raccoon] told me he didn't like the air freshener or being carried out by the tail," George laughed, adding a mouse ran up a pants' leg once at the Luray Full Gospel Church building.

Full Gospel continues Saturday night services, and Luray Baptist still meets on Sundays.

"People didn't think the two churches could get along. But we preach the same Jesus," George said of himself and Luray Baptist pastor Rex Link.

Now, most of the old guard at the church is long gone, and many of the Full Gospel service attendees have memberships in other churches.

Dozens of names fill George and Linda's memories with gratitude—family members, Lester Piersee, Harry Miller, Harold Shelton, Gene Spurgeon, Gene Baker, Don Waterman, Donnie Gillpin, Gary Whitaker, their parents, to name a few. Harold, Don, Donnie, and Gary and the parents plus many of the adults during George's childhood are enjoying their eternal reward with Jesus.

"I know the people that witnessed to me spoke the truth," George said.

The couple also has a special place in their hearts for the Gideons International in the work they do to put Bibles where they are easily accessible.

"I thank God for that day when God's Word literally leaped from a *little red book* lying there in the snow.

"And I want to thank the people of the Gideons Association for their dedication to the spreading of God's Word. Had that Bible not been purchased and placed, had it not been discarded, I would not be here. God does work in mysterious ways."

George sometimes quotes at least part of Isaiah 55:11, *"So shall my word be that goeth forth out of my mouth: it shall not return unto me void, but it shall accomplish that which I please, and it shall prosper in the thing whereto I sent it."*

The remarkable story about how George LeMaster Jr. was saved through a discarded Bible shows that even though the Bible was of little value to someone, that God was not done with its purpose yet.

"He gives us the darkness sometimes, so we can see the stars. The value of the Bible is not knowing it, but obeying it," he said.

As far as that one red New Testament itself, its whereabouts are not immediately known mid-2021. Don Waterman had it, and it went to fellow Gideon Jack Chapman, formerly of Clark County, Missouri, and more recently on Union, Missouri, who thought it was in the custody of the Nashville Headquarters. The Gideons' head-quarters could not confirm they had it.

"It did what it was supposed to do," George said, unconcerned about whether or not it will ever show up again.

George LeMaster Jr. is the type not to hold too tightly to things in this world, even a Bible that brought him to a saving knowledge of Jesus Christ.

"I have been sober these years since 1982 with no desire to drink. For the past thirty-four years [five less than saved], I've been the pastor of the Full Gospel Church [in Luray]. If I took a drink now, it would be like slapping God in the face for all he's done for me. I do not want to make him mad."

The place where George LeMaster Jr. first found the red-cov-ered Gideon New Testament—the Wayland dump—which was never in the city of Wayland, nor controlled by city officials, closed in the mid-1970s.

According to Mary Hopke, Environmental Supervisor for Compliance and Enforcement of the Missouri Department of Natural Resources in Jefferson City, the Wayland dump closed in 1976, and a number of others in Missouri were closed too.

She said an inspection by the Macon Office of the Department of Natural Resources—started just two years earlier—found it closed on July 22, 1976.

Trash from the Wayland community was then collected and sent to the MLS landfill near Canton, eighteen miles south. She said a city dump wasn't closed until another option for trash disposal is available. The MLS dump near Canton has since been closed too.

When the Wayland dump was closed, the junk steel was reportedly removed and sold to a scrapper. The rest of it was bulldozed in according to a city hall official. Since the dump was outside of the Wayland city limits, they had no legal control over it.

George Jr. said one reason the dump was closed was that area farmers were upset about small items, such as plastic bags, blowing out of the dump and jamming their farm equipment.

He happened to be there once when plastic bags from the dump littered across farmer Stewart Hagerman's bean field and got caught in the machine's blower. Hagerman reportedly had to tear down the combine in the field and spent better than four hours getting the bags out.

Standing in the pulpit at the Clark County Nursing Home circa 2015, George and other Golden Age Ministries band members played and sang some songs.

"Then I shared a word of God. There was Mrs. Lula Downing, my high school teacher from Revere. She was looking at me and smiling.

"We got done, and I was shaking hands with the residents. I stopped by Mrs. Downing, who was there because she couldn't care for herself. I said, 'I know what you are thinking.' She asked how I could know what she was thinking. I said, 'I know. It's the oral book reports.' She said, 'Mr. LeMaster, you remembered. You are speaking in public, but not as distinctly as I would have had you do.'

"Many stories have surfaced about my childhood [from nursing home residents] as I do meet people who have known me all my life.

"After Martha Coop [a neighbor from childhood] had a stroke, she couldn't talk well, but I'd say, 'We know where all the skeletons are, don't we?' She would nod *yes*."

Other childhood stories have come from other nursing home friends who were family friends or acquaintances when George was growing up, such as Mary Broomhall, whose late husband was among the toll bridge workers; Twila Peters, a longtime neighbor; the late Mary Alice Kinkeade, a fifth- and sixth-grade teacher; and the late Ida Daw, a first- and second-grade teacher at Wayland Public School 45.

All had talked about the good and bad years.

A favorite song of George's is "Where Could I Go?" The answer to that song question is *Jesus*.

Through a Gideon friend and two inmates at the Bowling Green Missouri prison, including his youngest son who did time for drug use, George was able to have the Gideons get Bibles to inmates.

"An inmate my wife and I corresponded with told us that Bibles were hard to obtain for inmates in prison. As a pastor, I talked to our Gideons representative and asked if he could talk to someone about getting Bibles for the prisoners. Money was given as a gift, and the Gideons did the rest. One case of Bibles was confirmed as received by our friend in prison."

Luray Full Gospel worship services are still on Saturday nights, but Bible study is now on Thursdays.

"Can't make it on Sundays? We are here on Saturdays. It's worked so far."

Like many other rural churches, the Luray Full Gospel Church is shrinking because older members are dying, and many younger families have moved from the community. George has pastored for nearly four decades with no formal Bible training. "Only what Harold Shelton taught me and on-the-job training."

He was hard-pressed to come up with just one or two ministry highlights.

"It has been one adventure after another. It has been a learning experience in dealing with people. The whole thing has been a highlight.

"I've done some counseling with ten or twelve people one-on-one. People who knew me, and *they* were to a place where they couldn't handle the alcohol anymore. They knew I would keep my mouth shut as a minister."

Also, many of those same people knew George LeMaster Jr.'s story, or at least that he was no longer an alcoholic.

"If I walk by a tavern now, it smells of stale beer and urine. I can't stand it. I used to think I was enjoying being in those places."

As this book is being written, a couple—said a long time ago to be too young for marriage—George and Linda LeMaster have celebrated fifty-six years of marriage and counting. They live in the same Wayland house on Des Moines Street they almost lost in his drinking days.

His sisters Connie and Colleen, now widows, and Martha, her husband Randy, and their children all live in Wayland. Another sister, Jeri Bradley, husband Kevin, and their daughter live in Centerville, Iowa.

George and Linda have seven grandchildren—Christina, Zachary, and Madison Wood; Jaden and Koby LeMaster; and Kara and Kyle Garrett. They have a great-grandson named Zadin Wood.

"The verses in James certainly have a spot with me, but I have found since that ALL the verses are my favorites," he said, adding he is partial to the Psalms and Proverbs.

Linda especially likes these verses:

I can do all things through Christ which strengthens me. (Philippians 4:13)

And whatsoever ye do in word or deed, do all in the name of the Lord Jesus, giving thanks to God and the Father by him. Wives, submit yourselves unto your own husbands, as it is fit in the Lord. Husbands, love your wives, and be not bitter against them. Children, obey your parents in all things: for this is well pleasing unto the Lord. Fathers, provoke not your children to anger, lest they be discouraged. (Colossians 3:17–21)

Therefore I say unto you, take no thought for your life, what ye shall eat, or what ye shall drink; nor yet for your body, what ye shall put on. Is not the life more than meat, and the body than raiment? Behold the fowls of the air: for they sow not, neither do they reap, nor gather into barns; yet your heavenly Father feedeth them. Are ye not much better than they? Which of you by taking thought can add one cubit unto his stature? And why take ye thought for raiment? Consider the lilies of the field, how they grow; they toil not, neither do they spin: And yet I say unto you, that even Solomon in all his glory was not arrayed like one of these. Wherefore, if God so clothe the grass of the field, which today is, and tomorrow is cast into the oven, shall he not much more clothe you, O ye of little faith?

(For after all these things do the Gentiles seek:) for your heavenly Father knoweth that Therefore, take no thought, saying, What shall we eat? or, What shall we drink? or, Wherewithal shall we be clothed? ye have need of all these things. But seek ye first the kingdom of God, and his righteousness; and all these things shall be added unto you. Take therefore no thought for the morrow: for the morrow shall take thought for the things of itself. Sufficient unto the day is the evil thereof. (Matthew 6:25–34)

Epilogue

I'm just a nobody
Telling everybody
About Somebody
Who can save anybody—Jesus
saves. Are you saved?

If you do not know Jesus Christ as your Savior, you can!

1. God knows you and loves you and has a plan for you.
   "For God so loved the world, that he gave his only begotten Son, that whosoever believeth in him should not perish, but have everlasting life" (John 3:16).
2. Man is sinful and separated from God.
   "For all have sinned, and come short of the glory of God" (Romans 3:23).
3. Sin has its price.
   "For the wages of sin is death; but the gift of God is eternal life through Jesus Christ our Lord" (Romans 6:23).
4. Jesus paid the price.
   "But God commendeth his love toward us, in that, while we were yet sinners, Christ died for us" (Romans 5:8).
5. Salvation is free.
   "For by grace are ye saved through faith; and that not of yourselves: it is the gift of God: Not of works, lest any man should boast" (Ephesians 2:8–9).
6. Each person must receive Jesus Christ.
   "Jesus saith unto him, I am the way, the truth, and the life: no man cometh unto the Father, but by me" (John 14:6).

Pray

"Heavenly Father, forgive me of my sins. Come into my life, Lord Jesus. Lord, I give myself to you. Help me to live for you. In Jesus's name. Amen."

If you made the decision to give your heart to Christ, find a body of believers to fellowship with, a Bible-believing church home, and read his Word daily. Remember James 4:7–10:

> *Submit yourselves therefore to God. Resist the devil, and he will flee from you. Draw nigh to God, and he will draw nigh to you. Cleanse your hands, ye sinners; and purify your hearts, ye double minded. Be afflicted, and mourn, and weep: let your laughter be turned to mourning, and your joy to heaviness. Humble yourselves in the sight of the Lord, and he shall lift you up.*

> *George W. LeMaster Jr.*

About the Author

Writing has long been a part of Dan Steinbeck's life. He has several decades of experience as a writer, editor, photographer, and publisher of a Lewis County, Missouri, newspaper and is blessed to have won several journalism contest awards. The family sold the newspaper in 2010. Through this experience, he has learned writing in various genres.

He believes everyone has a story.

He freelances for other publications including *The Pathway*, the official news journal of the Missouri Baptist Convention and *Missouri Life* magazine. He previously published *Nuts Squirrels and Knotholes in the Family Tree*, a book of Steinbeck family stories in 2013. He has a strong interest in museums, especially those in Missouri, and has written about some of these.

Steinbeck became a Christian at age ten. He began pastoring Southern Baptist Fellowship Church in Wayland, Missouri in 2001 and it was through a Bible study at this church Dan met George and Linda LeMaster and learned the fascinating story of God's deliverance.

He is also a driver for OATS public transit, a Missouri transportation network.

Steinbeck and his wife of thirty-five years, Carla, have two grown children, son Andrew "Will" Steinbeck and wife Julie; and daughter Shannon Steinbeck and a granddaughter Maria Steinbeck.

He is a lifelong resident of Lewis County, Missouri, and has served on the Lewis County Ambulance board and is currently a second-ward alderman with the city of Canton, Missouri.

CPSIA information can be obtained
at www.ICGtesting.com
Printed in the USA
BVHW050820220822
645037BV00002B/15